The Heart is a Funny Reservoir

A ROMANTIC ICELANDIC MEMOIR

By
Ed Chalom

PublishAmerica
Baltimore

© 2004 by Ed Chalom.

All rights reserved. No part of this book may be reproduced, stored in a retrieval system or transmitted in any form or by any means without the prior written permission of the publishers, except by a reviewer who may quote brief passages in a review to be printed in a newspaper, magazine or journal.

First printing

ISBN: 1-4137-1954-6
PUBLISHED BY PUBLISHAMERICA, LLLP
www.publishamerica.com
Baltimore

Printed in the United States of America

DEDICATION

*To Ragnheider Ingvarsdottir,
who shared with me these improbable memories*

ACKNOWLEDGEMENTS

I would like to thank Willem Meiners for encouraging me to tell my Icelandic story, and also my daughters Eve Chalom and Melanie Goldberg and my friends Harriet Maza and Bob Mantell for their down-to-earth advice.

TABLE OF CONTENTS

Prologue
Ragnheider Ingvarsdottir 11

Chapter One
The Role of a Supply Sergeant 14

Chapter Two
20,000 Military Personnel 19

Chapter Three
Her Name Was 23

Chapter Four
We Met at a Dance 26

Chapter Five
A Simple Icelandic Fisherman 30

Chapter Six
Furlough Time 35

Chapter Seven
We Have Loved 40

Chapter Eight
A Beautiful Auburn-Haired Nurse 44

Chapter Nine
 One Brief Summer 47

Chapter Ten
 Linguistically Compatible 51

Chapter Eleven
 Scotland and England 55

Chapter Twelve
 Dottie and I Parted 59

Chapter Thirteen
 48 Years 63

Chapter Fourteen
 The Heart is a Funny Reservoir 66

Ragnheider's Epilogue
 His Name Was 71

La misma noche que hace blanquear los mismos arboles.
Nosotros, los de entonces, ya no somos los mismos.

Ya no la quiero, es cierto, pero cuánto la quise.
Mi voz buscaba el viento para tocar su oído.

De otro. Será de otro. Como antes de mis besos.
Su voz, su cuerpo claro. Sus ojos infinitos.

Ya no la quiero, es cierto, pero tal vez la quiero.
Es tan corto el amor, y es tan largo el olvido.

De: *Puedo escribir los versos mas triste esta noche*
Por Pablo Neruda

                The same night that whitens the same trees.
                  We, of that time, are no longer the same.

I no longer love her, that's certain, but, oh, how I loved her.
        My voice searched for the wind to touch her hearing.

      Another's. She will be another's. Like before my kisses.
             Her voice, her bright body. Her infinite eyes.

   I no longer love her, that's certain, but maybe I love her.
          Love is so short, and forgetting is so long.

                    From: *Tonight I can write the saddest lines*
              By: Pablo Neruda (translation: Ed Chalom)

Ragnheider Ingvasdottir

Prologue
RAGNHEIDER INGVARSDOTTIR

"We have loved more in one brief summer than most people have loved in all their lives. Oh, how I wish you were a simple Icelandic fisherman so that you could stay with me rather than fly away." It was September 1955, and I received this letter shortly after my departure from Iceland. The deceptively named island in the north Atlantic had been my theatre of operations for a year and I had played the role of supply sergeant. At that time there were over 20,000 military personnel stationed at Keflavik Air Base located about 30 miles from the capital city of Reykjavik, but very few like me who took an interest in the country or its people.

Her name was Ragnheider Ingvarsdottir – Dottie for short. She was a beautiful auburn-haired nurse. She worked in a city hospital and we met at a dance fairly early in my stay, although our lives didn't intertwine until my last three months there. Her semi-fluent English was comparable to my semi-fluent Icelandic, so we were linguistically compatible aside from other compatibilities. When I was up for some furlough time, I took her to Scotland and England, which provided her with her first experience of the world outside of Iceland. The highlight of her trip was, I imagine, the afternoon spent shopping the big London department stores.

The memory is a funny kind of reservoir. There is sometimes no logical reason why certain things are quickly effaced and others stubbornly stick. Dottie and I parted. The probability of our lives ever crossing again was practically nil. Our stars followed different trajectories in different parts of the universe with no intergalactic communication. And yet *48 years later*, when my daughter Eve suggested that we take a vacation together in Iceland and I had agreed, the submerged, stubbornly sticking details surfaced. How can one forget a name like Ragnheider Ingvarsdottir? But many other images of our distant encounter materialized. I was ready to go back to Iceland in

June 2003, but the trip had now assumed an unexpected emotional dimension. Not only was I going back geographically, but I was going back to my past life and I wasn't sure of what I would find.

Icelanders use a patronymic system for naming their children; you are somebody's son or somebody's daughter (dottir), but the handy thing is that women do not change their names when married. A woman is forever her father's daughter, never her husband's wife. Phone book white pages list people by their first names first. There are about 275,000 Icelanders on the island and they are all on the national database with name, address, phone number and date of birth. Six Ragnheider Ingvarsdottirs popped up on the computer screen at the hotel information desk. Three were quickly eliminated because of the age factor. I reached two others by phone and verified that they were not the person I was looking for. The last possible woman had an inoperable phone because the number had been put "in storage," a system permitting a person to disconnect the phone but reserve the number for future use. Well, I had the address, so I decided to make a personal appearance.

It was a neat complex of two-story apartment buildings and a woman in the parking lot pointed out the correct unit. There were four apartments in the unit and the lit doorbell of one flashed "Ragnheider Ingvarsdottir." I held my breath and pushed the button. Who would walk through the door? Had she been waiting for my return? Would she even remember me?

There was no answer. I then noticed that her mailbox was stuffed with letters and papers indicating it had not been emptied for some time. I left a note: *My name is Ed Chalom. I was a soldier stationed at Keflavik in 1955, and I had a friend named Ragnheider Ingvarsdottir. I don't know if you are that same woman. You can reach me at...*

According to a recent census, there are 73,165 horses in Iceland. They are a unique breed of horse and Eve was eager to ride. We were planning to go to a large stable for a group ride but at the last minute I decided it would be preferable to go to a smaller stable on our own. Two lady riders went out with us on the trails through the lava field and in conversation with one I found out that she was the director of nurses at the main Reykjavik hospital.

"Is it possible that you know a nurse, probably retired, by the name of Ragnheider Ingvarsdottir?"

"No, but I have a complete directory at the hospital of all past and present Icelandic nurses. After our ride we'll go to the hospital and check it out."

At the hospital, the director drew down the three-volume directory of nurses and there on the bottom of a page of R's was Ragnheider Ingvarsdottir with the same birthdate as the woman with the "in storage" telephone. There was a full paragraph outlining her life story and when we turned the page her serene clear-eyed photo looked out at me. Among the details of her education, work history and lineage was the fact that she had married an American sailor in 1959. They had had one son and sometime thereafter had been divorced. She retired as a nurse in 1989. It struck me as somehow sad to see her life summarized in a paragraph as, indeed, my own life similarly could be reduced to a few words and numbers.

Iceland is a volcanic island where hot water for heating and swimming surges out of underground springs. On our next to last day in Reykjavik we made our daily visit to one of the ubiquitous swimming pools. This Arbaerjarlaug pool is located near Dottie's apartment. Impelled by my genetic persistence, I decided that since I knew where the right woman lived, I could find out more information about her absence from one of her neighbors.

"Do you speak English?"

"Yes."

"Do you know Ragnheider Ingvarsdottir?"

"She doesn't live here."

"But her name is right there on the door bell!"

"Oh, but she is living in Spain now. Every year she lives in Spain for six or seven months and then she comes back."

Our days died imperceptibly – day is day and night is day in the Icelandic June.

We arrived at the airport a couple hours before flight time, passed through security and were waiting at the gate when a voice on the loudspeaker said, "Would passenger Edward Chalom please come to the information desk in the main terminal."

"Eve, watch the baggage and I'll go see what they want."

As I approached the information desk a white-haired graceful lady turned to face me.

"Hello, Eddie. Long time no see."

The heart is a funny reservoir. From the depth of an inexpressible emotion, tears leaped to our eyes. We touched hands and stood there weeping senselessly.

The flight back was silent and uneventful.

Chapter One
THE ROLE OF A SUPPLY SERGEANT

"You're a fool! You'll just be another number to them. You're a damn fool if you let them draft you into the Army when you can get out of it. You don't have to go. This guy can pull the right strings."

"But, Ma, I don't feel right about being a draft dodger."

"*Aennaa,* draft dodger, your cousin Joe spent the whole Second World War in Mexico but at least he came back alive and now he has a good business."

It was early 1953, and the Korean War was winding down although the truce talks were hung up on the voluntary repatriation of the prisoners of war. I was a 21-year-old idealist that had done my bit to avoid the military draft by joining the New York State National Guard two years earlier. The Guard was a play Army where you spent a couple hours a week at a downtown armory where you metamorphosed into military uniform, shuffled some papers, had a snack, earned a few bucks and occasionally a promotion stripe. Two weeks a year you went to camp to do KP, polish weapons of individual destruction and pick up pine needles when the commanding officer thought the forest was too messy.

Selective Service subsequently eliminated the draft exemption for National Guard service and here I was facing a two-year stint in the full-time regular Army. I felt screwed post de facto but then the law is the law and there was always the image in Technicolor of my patriotic duty.

"At least let me ask him over and listen to his offer, otherwise it's two years out of your life."

"Ok, but I still don't like the idea of buying my way out."

He was a plump, balding Syrian with a seven o'clock shadow and slits for eyes and when he sat on the couch he sort of rolled back into a resting position and lit a cigarette.

"It's really basically a simple set-up. Just follow my instructions and you'll be out in less than a month."

"What do I have to do?"

"When you get drafted they'll send you to Fort Dix in New Jersey. From the minute you get there you act like a *meshnoon*, you know, sort of crazy. You don't talk to anybody, don't respond to anybody, don't recognize anybody, stop eating. Within a week they'll send you to the base hospital. That's where we have some of the doctors paid off to issue you a medical discharge. That's where part of your 'consulting' fee goes. If you're lucky you may be able to get a lifetime disability pension after your month's service. You won't be the only one in the community doing this."

I had grown up on the streets of Brooklyn but certainly not in a world of gang wars, drugs, pimps or poverty. The community of Sephardic Jews which had emigrated from Syria in the early years of the 20th century was very close-knit. It was a sort of village life sandwiched in the midst of a great metropolis. Arabic was frequently spoken and even English dialogue was seasoned with Semitic expressions. They referred to themselves as SYs to distinguish themselves from the "J-Dubs" or Ashkenazi Jews of eastern European origins. As with many ethnic minorities, a certain elite status was implied by the use of these distinguishing labels. The Judaism followed was nominally orthodox, an orthodoxy tempered with a wink and a shrug. I was a willing disciple, accepting unquestioningly the rote learning funneled into me from the age of four.

It was into this Brooklyn village that my mother arrived from Aleppo at the age of seven. Even at that age, Alberta was known for her unusual beauty. She eventually attracted the adoration of a well-to-do diamond merchant, Ezekhiel Chalom, and a marriage arranged in heaven was formalized on earth in the section of Brooklyn called Bensonhurst. He was 45. She was 14.

I never saw my father. Within the first year of their marriage Alberta had borne my brother Hy and was already pregnant with me when my father was shot and killed. He had struggled with an armed intruder who had broken into the house and he died in this instinctive but foolish show of bravery. Several months later I was born in that same house. At the age of 15 my mother was a widow and single parent of two infant boys.

"No, I think I prefer to do my time in service. Who knows, it might be a good experience and at least there's no hot war going on. Thanks for stopping by."

"No problem. You can let me know if you change your mind."

Education was not the raison d'etre of the SY community. The main criterion of worth was the quantity of accumulated wealth. Sons were oriented towards entering family businesses mainly in wholesale and retail soft goods. Daughters were groomed for advantageous marriages. The fact that my father was in the diamond business was an anomaly. Very few pursued college studies but in my teenage years I entertained ideas of breaking out of the typical mold.

I had been able to experience a year of full-time college because I had graduated from high school at the age of 15 and my mother agreed that I could delay the start of my business career. Brooklyn College was conveniently located and even after my one year as a full-time student I continued attending night courses.

After my life as a full-time student ended, I was employed as a courier/office boy for a cousin in the diamond business at a salary of $22 a week. When it became clear that the opportunity for growth in this position was extremely limited, I shifted to wholesale selling for another relative importing infants wear handmade in the Philippines. I merchandised our line through stores like Macy's, W.T. Grant and SS Kresge. I was successful there and stayed with the job until I received my draft notice. I took two weeks off before being inducted to hitchhike at random down the East Coast. My mother said, "Our people don't do that." The first lift took me to Atlantic City, the second to Washington D.C. I was just getting the feel of stretching my wings.

It was a bitterly cold winter in the northeastern U.S. the winter of 1953, when I arrived at Fort Dix, New Jersey, for 16 weeks of basic training. When I entered the mess hall on my first day in camp I saw my childhood buddy, Nate Dweck, serving food behind the hot table. We had been in Hebrew school together and played a zillion innings of stickball afterwards. In the summer we had both bantered with the girls on the beach in New Jersey.

"Nate, what's happening, man!" He silently gazed through me as if I were transparent. Nate had become a *meshnoon*.

Carrying my rank from the National Guard, I entered the regular army as a sergeant but went through all the basic training with all the other draftees and recruits. I was probably the most easygoing sergeant the base had ever seen. Having risen in the ranks through a relatively short-cut route, I still had a civilian mentality with little enthusiasm for the gung-ho bullshit that made up so much of the busy work of the military. I did benefit from the physical conditioning, I could run continuously for five miles with a full pack on my back. After basic training, I was appointed supply sergeant at the same basic training company where I had been trained. My supply room was run honestly and I refused to participate in the general thievery of government material.

"Sergeant Chalom, you're assigned to do the head count at the mess hall for this week. You'll be at the mess hall before each meal and count the number of guys we feed."

"Yes, sir."

I did the job meticulously, counting all the GIs we fed during the week and noting the numbers on the tally sheet. At the end of the week, when the mess sergeant presented me with the tally sheets to sign, I was amazed to see he had just about doubled all my figures.

"I won't sign off on those trumped-up numbers."

"Fuck it, I'll get someone else to sign."

He made a bundle selling the excess food requisitioned in the nearby town. They never asked me to do the head count again.

Enlisted men were housed in large two-story barracks but non-commissioned officers like sergeants and corporals were assigned rooms instead of sleeping in the large open areas. I shared a room with Corporal Green, a hulking black, gentle giant. In the SY community, blacks were referred to as *abeed* which translates literally into the word "slave" and the only social interchange was as employer to maid. Green was my assistant in the supply room and was always very accommodating. Although he was over six feet and seventy pounds heavier than me, we would occasionally have friendly wrestling matches in our room. What I lacked in size and strength I made up for in speed and agility. We noisily smashed into walls and furniture and strained and sweated. We found it hilarious. His skin color didn't rub off on my skin nor mine

Shipping out to Iceland

on his.

After 11 months at Fort Dix, I received my orders for overseas duty. Great! I had actually been looking forward to an interesting foreign tour of duty.

The orders did not even include an illustrated travel folder – they stipulated in officialese that I would spend the second year of my military career at the military base at Keflavik, Iceland. Oh no! Not Iceland! What's the possibility of getting my destination changed to Germany, France, Hawaii? No way. Iceland. Even the name shook me up.

Chapter Two
20,000 MILITARY PERSONNEL

I was, of course, wrong, wrong, wrong. This was not a country of igloos, Eskimos, and polar bears. Whether mistranslated from the Norse word for island or so named to frighten off invaders, Iceland was populated by about 200,000 Nordic people, handsome and highly literate. Although Iceland is at a higher latitude than Ft. Dix, New Jersey, where I had endured a severe winter during my basic training, the climate in Iceland was surprisingly milder. This is due to the effects of the Gulf Stream which brings warmer currents across the Atlantic to break upon the southern and western Icelandic shores. The temperature in southern Iceland never gets colder than plus 30 degrees Fahrenheit, even in winter. That is not to say the weather is balmy. The central highlands have an Arctic climate and the collision of the polar and temperate air can result in heavy winds and rapid weather changes.

The value of what you get out of any situation depends largely on how much you bring to it. It's as true in travel, as it is in literature, theatre or friendships. I started to read all I could find about this unknown country and even began to study the unique Old Norse language still spoken there. My initial despair evolved into curiosity.

The military transport plane that carried us there had benches that ran the length of the body on each side. Comfort was definitely a secondary consideration and the flight offered no business-class option. We stopped off at Goose Bay, Labrador, a desolate land that may have been a welcomed sight for Leif Eriksson but for us suggested a forbidding prelude of what was awaiting us. After refueling, we flew on to Iceland. The wind was howling at 80 miles an hour that dark November morning when we taxied to a stop at the Keflavik Air Force Base. Portable stairs were rolled up to the plane. Two hefty men had to lean all their weight against the swing-out door before it would open and a woman, buried in a parka, blew into the plane shouting breathlessly, "Welcome to Iceland."

We might have mistakenly landed on the moon judging from the barren, stony landscape that stared at us to which we returned our own stony stares. Iceland was, in fact, an astronaut training area for the moon landing. The terminal building was not much larger than a double Quonset hut, although it did have a small gift shop selling woolen sweaters and tourist trinkets. We weren't in a buying mood. Busses hauled us and our duffel bags to our new home – a series of long, gray concrete three-story buildings.

Each room accommodated two and was furnished with two beds and two clothes lockers. That was it. The communal bathroom in the center of the hall served the entire floor housing about 60 men. About 70 percent of the troops were draftees, the rest regular Army, which included some "lifers." My roommate was RA Staff Sergeant Dixon, like me, in the supply section, and who already was in the active business of selling handsome dark blue Air Force parkas. He also made gifts of them to some of his superior officers such as our commanding officer Captain Gullekson. I knew of only one officer, Warrant Officer Andrews, who refused the pilfered parkas. RA Dixon came from Alabama and on his wall calendar he was already counting down the days of his return to his hot, sunny paradise. Talking to someone like Dixon, an RA from the South, was like trying to bridge the cultural gap dividing a believer and a non-believer. The distance between Brooklyn and Alabama is measured in more than miles. We generally went our separate ways.

"We are blessed. We are truly blessed." Wrapped in his Army blanket standing outside the barracks in the blustery night, Corporal Madden gazed up at the northern lights that danced in the black sky. I had never seen these mostly green, ghostlike glowing forms and I was also in awe. "Yes, we are truly blessed to have seen this magnificent aurora borealis." Actually, he had been less than blessed in his army career of 20 years, having been broken down from master sergeant to corporal due to his alcoholism. But his cavernous cheeks emitted a deep, refined voice extolling his appreciation of the natural wonders of the world. His whole adult life had been dedicated to the military and I commiserated that his punctilious posture and polish was now simply a façade to conceal his failure. He stood like a forlorn Indian lost in the pyrotechnics of the firmament.

Private Henderson from Chicago and I had the same bemused attitude toward the standard operating procedures that ruled all activities in the military mind. He was a reader and a lover of classical music, two things that didn't conform to the norm in those barracks. We had interesting conversations; although, typically, sergeants did not fraternize with privates. It was sometimes a challenge, but frequently rewarding, to get to know the person behind the uniform. When he addressed me as Sergeant Chalom, he would stress the word *Sergeant*, giving it a respectful, hallowed connotation that made us both laugh at its pomposity.

The great majority of the military personnel never left the base to see the rest of the island. Reykjavik, which they had difficulty pronouncing correctly, was referred to as "Rinky Dink." Their generic term for the Icelandic people was "fishheads." This did not impede, however, the flow of trade between some soldiers who bought things like watches, clothing and diamond rings at low PX prices and sold them in Rinky Dink at a good profit.

I read in the base newsletter that an instructor would be coming out to the base twice a week to give lessons in the Icelandic language. I signed up. Out of the 20,000 military personnel on the base, I was the only one who showed up for the class. There was one other student, an American civilian. Mac was a construction worker who had been in Iceland for three years and had been studying Icelandic on his own. Smiling Mac and I were great friends, meeting in and out of class to practice Icelandic during the week. This friendship continued even after he attempted an amorous advance. When his hand crept up my thigh, I simply made it clear I was not on his sexual wavelength. He backed off immediately.

Construction never seemed to end on this base. The workers were a hardy lot, some Americans and mostly Icelanders. At this time of the year it was mostly dark and nasty but they strung up lights, pulled on boots and gloves and pounded away. Our Icelandic instructor, Thor Thorlafson, reminded me of the hardy, local kids that played outside in all types of weather. His youthful, rosy cheeks and light blue eyes belied the fact that he was about 60 and chain-smoked. I looked on him as both a linguistic and cultural link. We would meet in town occasionally to share the local chicory-laced coffee which I hated, or a bowl of skyr, a unique, thick, sweet yogurt which I adored.

There was another notice of interest in the newsletter. There would be a weekly dance on the base for the enlisted men. Girls from Reykjavik would be bussed in on Thursday nights. I awaited these dances with great anticipation. Public busses were just about the only mode of transportation besides walking, and there was a regular schedule to and from town.

By the end of the second week, however, my ship had come in – the ship, that is, that the Army used, thanks to my rank, to bring my car from the States to Iceland. It was a green 1952 Chevrolet that fired right up on the dock as soon as the cables were reattached to the battery. It gave me a mobility and a sense of independence that was not afforded most of the other soldiers. The New York car and I were unaccustomed to the bumpy dirt roads and the foreign road signs of Iceland, but in time, we found our way around. The only paved roads in the country were in the city of Reykjavik and on the base at Keflavik and I had to order heavy-duty replacement tires from the Sears catalog within a month. I had to learn how to drive on these only occasionally graded roads; too slowly and the car fell into every depression; too fast and the car would skim many low spots but hit the peaks with too much force. The road mandated moderation. It was understood that the road between Keflavik and Reykjavik, although fairly heavily traveled, remained unpaved to discourage fraternization between the Americans and the Icelanders.

Well, I was one American that was ready and eager to fraternize.

Chapter Three
HER NAME WAS

Non-contractual copulation was not common in the Sephardic community of Brooklyn. If you wanted to get laid, you first got married or at least engaged. The young ladies could and did engage in promiscuous verbal intercourse but societal pressures assured *coitus interruptus* before any *coitus* took place. Not only was pre-marital sex rare, but divorce was practically unheard of. A divorced woman was the ultimate fallen woman with no value in the marriage marketplace. Within the village mentality that existed, everybody knew everything about everybody – the family origins and the complete family tree, the business successes and failures, who went out with whom and why. Things were also positively known that were, in reality, not so.

Her name was Elba Maldonado. She and I both worked at the same infants wear company, she in the processing plant and I in sales, although I frequently helped out in the plant. The work force of about a dozen women who ironed and attached ornaments to the infants wear were all Puerto Rican or Dominican and the Spanish babbling brooked no end. I had studied Spanish in college and I was soon fluent. Being exposed to Arabic in my youth had opened my mind to readily accepting and processing other foreign languages.

Woody Allen in his wisdom once said, "The main advantage of being bisexual is that it doubles your chances for a Saturday night date." Being bilingual also serves the same purpose. It broadens your options. The promotion of this fact would be a wonderful way to motivate apathetic high school students in their foreign language studies. Besides Woody Allen, King Alfonso the Wise of Spain, over 700 years ago, figured that a person that could speak two languages was worth two people and he rewarded his translators accordingly.

Elba was from San Juan. She and I talked. Her petite frame was covered with very fair skin crowned by wavy light brown hair. She stood very close to me in the crowded elevator after work. In fact, I stood looking straight ahead in my blue business suit with one hand clutching the *New York Times* and the other feeling her smooth ass. We met in upper Manhattan and went to the movies. As we sat necking in the balcony, she smoothly loosened the belt of her skirt and let my hand slide inside her panties. And on the first date! This had never happened in my other Latino-deprived life. When we walked out of the theatre the heavens poured out a veritable deluge, an evident sign of God's wrath.

"Birds do it, bees do it, even monkeys in the trees do it, Let's do it...." At this point in my life, I was not too preoccupied with making fine distinctions between lust and love. Chastity and virginity had been successfully marketed to me for several years as the greatest gift you could bring your wife. But this concept had been recently shattered when a chaste young thing told me that she would prefer a husband who was not a virgin, a man with more experience than she. Well, now!

I had certainly been attracted to several of the young ladies of my milieu. Sometimes they were ethereal, pedestal loves, other times somewhat more physical. Our crowd was very much into couple dancing so touching was not taboo. But there is touching and then there is *touching*, and with Elba, I was now facing the ultimate physicality.

Birds, bees, and monkeys may go to it quite naturally but Elba and I, both of us unschooled, had a hell of a time figuring out exactly where and how to do it. Using first a concealed doorway, then the back seat of a borrowed car and finally Prospect Park after a band concert, we eventually aligned our organs for compatible copulative positions. She had moved from upper Manhattan to live with relatives in Brooklyn, which made it more convenient, and our weekly assignations, secret for her as well as for me, were as strong an attraction as an open flame to moths. At work we maintained an air of polite indifference. On the weekends we had protected sex. Her Spanglish words whispered, "Eduardo, to me you are pleasing; from the first minute, I put my heart in you." We escaped being burned but after a year her parents ordered her back to Puerto Rico and that spelled *el fin* to our relationship. It had been a pleasant, sexual interlude in a Romance language but, for me, it had never blossomed romantically. The vast majority of my social life was still within the SY community.

At one time my heart had galloped after gorgeous Silvia Sutton, but she was married off to a wealthy family even before she was old enough to be allowed out on dates. Norma Masleton harshly spurned my youthful crush in favor of the handsome son of a rabbi. Now at this time, Marilyn Sultan had been my virginal SY girlfriend for some time but it was understood that we lived in the chastity belt section of the country. She was bright, educated and spoiled. We took piano lessons from the same teacher. Our extended after-party conversations sometimes welcomed in the dawn. Her round face and round bosom gave her an attractiveness that could not exactly be described as beauty. There was no question that we shared the same cultural roots and knew crowds of the same people.

"I haven't mentioned this to you before, Marilyn, but there is a strong probability that I'll be drafted into the Army."

"What does that mean?"

"It means that I'll be a soldier for two years and there's no telling where I'll be stationed."

"But what does that mean for us?"

"It means that for two years we wouldn't be seeing very much of each other. No regular Saturday night dates. No pick-up dance parties."

"That would be tough. I wouldn't like it but if I knew there was a commitment between us I would be willing to wait. I would wait for you."

My response was silence. I feared starting a progression of implicit understandings that would take on a life of its own would be impossible or painful to disavow. The path was smoothly paved and tempting to step on but I was not ready.

I had not been entirely comfortable leading a double love life but I didn't see any alternative within the context of this society if I wanted to satisfy both my social and physical desires. And I wanted to. Besides, the element of risk made it all the more *piquante*. In addition, it gave me a broader range of experiences with different types of people.

Meanwhile I was in the second month of another liaison dangereuse with a Latin lover which ended abruptly when Uncle Sam interrupted my dalliance to put me through military training and subsequently ship me overseas. By the time I reached Iceland my sexual experiences had brought my lovemaking to about the sensual sensitivity of that of birds, bees or monkeys. I looked forward to complementing my soldiering skills with an exploration of Scandinavian-style love.

But Ragnheider Ingvarsdottir was still at a distance in my Icelandic future.

Chapter Four
WE MET AT A DANCE

I always felt like I came out of the womb dancing. I was good at it because it was a love relationship – foxtrot, swing, rumba, mambo, samba, waltz, tango, even international folk dancing and flamenco. But the dancing of my youth and adulthood was interactive, free style, always with a touch of romance. Dance without romance was dance by patterns and numbers, a colorless combination. The twenty-first century terpsichoreal gymnastics may excel in individual virtuosity but they lack the warmth and closeness of ballroom dancing. Birthday parties, weddings, bar mitzvahs, spontaneous pick-up parties in my youth all centered around dancing. I found that dance is simply another language, a body language, that complements being bilingual as the most effective way to attract and hold girlfriends. Even tough guys can learn how to dance.

But have you ever danced in combat boots? In Iceland, enlisted men were required to be in full uniform both on and off base. It was a challenge to glide and float like Fred Astaire with five-pound weights on each foot. It may have been harder to dance but we danced.

"How long have you been in Iceland?"

"This is only my second week."

"Oh you're a newcomer. Welcome to our country."

"Thanks for your hospitality."

"And what do you think of our country?"

"Well, it's a little too soon to pass judgment but I think I'm going to like it."

"Even the weather? I hate the Icelandic winter, so dark, so rainy, so windy."

"*Ekki belja.*"

"*Ekki belja?!*"

She cracked up. She was laughing so hard she had to stop dancing. Unexpectedly hearing Icelandic words coming out of my mouth, even though incorrectly used, had the power to break glacial ice. I had just wanted to say something like "don't complain" but my words meant "no bellowing."

Her name was Bibi. She wore a beige knit wool dress that clung to her form, highlighting nicely her small but pointy breasts. Her smooth forehead flowed into a pert nose between smiling tawny eyes. Bibi was light on her feet but clearly had not been exposed to much variety in social dancing. She had an unusual way of standing with her arms akimbo, legs planted wide, pelvis tilted back. I found out later that when she stood erect her Mound of Venus was so prominent it caused a bulge in the front of her skirt which she found embarrassing. In effect, she was holding herself like a man attempting to suavely conceal an erection.

Aside from the weekly dance on base, Bibi informed me that there were regular dances held in Reykjavik on the weekend. These were all Icelandic dances where the GIs were a decided minority. I wondered what kind of reception we Americans would receive from the Icelandic men. Would they feel we were invading their territory and stealing their women? The presence of the military base in their country was not welcomed in all sectors of the political spectrum. There was a small but voluble Communist Party, whose daily newspaper *Tjodvillin*, regularly demanded an end to the American occupation of Keflavik. At these dances there was no possibility of just melting into the crowd, dressed as we were in military uniforms.

But the base had been there over a dozen years by now and it was generally accepted. Certainly, many appreciated the economic spillover and employment opportunities presented by the U.S. military establishment. There was little industry employment aside from the fishing industry. Iceland had no army of its own and very few policemen were needed to fight the practically non-existent crime.

It was at a Reykjavik dance at the end of my first month in Iceland that I first met Ragnheider Ingvarsdottir. As the music played and we swayed, we traded repartee.

"Do you live and work in Reykjavik?"

"Yes, but I was born and grew up in a small town named Patreksfjordur in the north of the country."

"And what kind of work do you do?"

"I graduated last year as a *hjukrunarkona,* a nurse, and I'm working at the Solheima clinic. My sister and I each have small apartments just a five-minute walk to my work."

"What kind of patients does this clinic handle?"

"We take care of woman problems."

"That's funny, I have woman problems. Maybe you can help me."

"I don't think we are talking about the same kind of problems. But what about you? How long have you been here?

"Just about one month."

"And how do you like Iceland?"

"Well, for me, a country is its people more so than its cities or mountains or lakes. And the more people like you that I can meet the more I like it."

"Aren't you the smooth talker."

Our light repartee continued, exploring other facets of the American-Icelandic connection. Her quiet beauty and relaxed laugh floated into the reservoir of my memory. She had been through professional training and seemed intelligent without trying to impress. From this pleasant enough beginning, things between Ragnheider Ingvarsdottir and me might have progressed to a closer relationship but a certain train of events conspired to derail our incipient romance.

One had to do with Bibi and the other with the Icelandic Communist Party. The party had organized a general strike throughout the country and one result of this action was that all military leaves off base were cancelled. I lost contact with all my acquaintances in Reykjavik. Mr. Thorlofsson was the only acquaintance that was allowed on base so at least Mac and I were able to continue our lessons in Icelandic. But Bibi searched me out. Although she was not allowed on base, one night she took the bus which brought her to the camp gates. There I met her and we made love in my car which was parked in the darkness beside the guard post. It was awkward and she got a big bump on her head climbing into the back seat but she said it was worth it. But that only happened once, after which even that short release was denied us. We could only maintain contact sporadically by phone.

The strike continued for almost two months which was a period of utter frustration because I had had only a brief voluptuous taste of the fulfillment I knew was awaiting me on the other side of the fence. And every night the base radio station would play two songs that fueled my frustration. One was "Kiss me once and kiss me twice and kiss me once again. It's been a long, long time." The second one, which was the sign-off song right before the national anthem, crooned "Mr. Sandman, send me a dream. Make her the cutest that I've ever seen." Yeah, right.

The Heart is a Funny Reservoir

Bibi lived in a small town the Keflavik side of Reykjavik, a town called Hafnarfjordur which is easier to get to than it is to pronounce. She had a cottage that she shared with her mother and sister and she had invited me to live with them on the weekends. It appeared that our relationship was entering a more intimate phase. When the strike finally ended, I accepted her enticing invitation and entered into a new phase of understanding about the personal life of Icelanders.

Chapter Five
A SIMPLE ICELANDIC FISHERMAN

"And the first grey of dawning filled the east" and a strange smell rose up over the land. Fish was the mainstay of the Icelandic diet and the Icelandic economy and evidence of it surrounded us. Keflavik was basically a fishing village and the military base was a couple of miles north of the town. I visited a fish plant there and watched as dexterous women slit, gutted, scaled and guillotined fish carcasses feeding down a conveyor belt. Definitely not the aquarium variety I used to keep at home.

Out in the fresh air, the odor of drying codfish was everywhere. Hanging from acres of wood racks the cod bodies swung in the wind like lynch victims effusing an odor combining the seashore and roasted nuts. It wasn't bad. When completely dried the *fiskibrot* or fish bread was rock hard and odorless. It had a shelf life of about one hundred years. But it was the kind of thing that I could store in my clothes locker without danger of detection. By simply breaking off a piece and masticating patiently for a few minutes one could soften the fish and release the pungent oily flavor. We were fed dinner about 5:30 p.m. and when I was ravenous at 10:00 p.m., a piece of dehydrated fiskibrot was a satiating salvation. I also tried stocking crackers and Icelandic blue cheese in my locker but after a couple days the odor permeated the corridor attracting hungry late nighters. But nobody ever asked for fiskibrot. I once tasted cured or rotted shark meat that had been buried in sand and brine for two years but I couldn't say that it was something that I afterwards hungered for.

The national strike finally ended and we were again allowed to leave the base from 6 p.m. to midnight weekdays and after noon Saturday until midnight Sunday. Accepting Bibi's seductive offer to spend the weekends at her house opened a new cultural and practical challenge for me. Would her mother and older sister object? How would they look upon me? Where would I sleep?

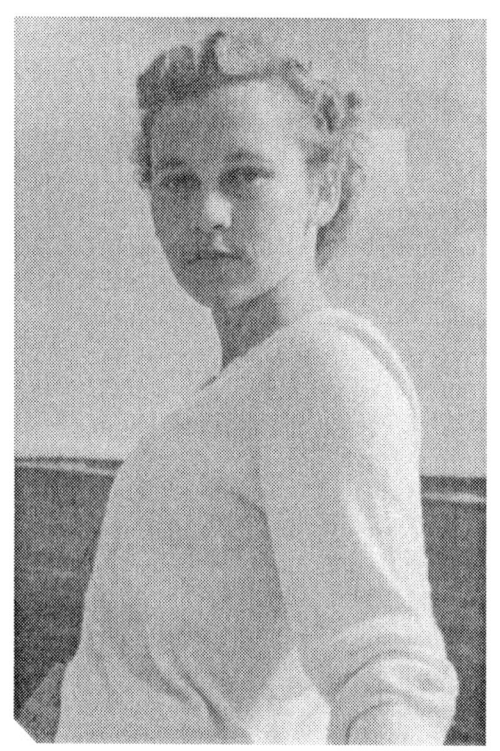

Bibi

    I quickly realized that Icelanders had a much more liberal attitude toward man-woman relations than I had been accustomed to in Brooklyn. Repression was not part of their amorous vocabulary. Sexual intercourse was entered into more freely without a sense of guilt or concealment. A couple who had found favor in each other's eyes could shortly begin cohabiting with family approval, sometimes even in the home of one of the families. Illegitimate children bore no stigma; in fact, the word illegitimate had no meaning when applied to human beings. Such children were absorbed into families and nurtured as warmly as those born within wedlock. Mothers in the States, however, wouldn't consider it nurturing to allow small children to play outdoors in rainy gales or blizzards but the well-bundled, red-cheeked, happy little elves seemed to thrive.

    I was accepted as a weekend family member of the household. Bibi and I slept in the combination bedroom-living room and her mother slept on the other side of a sliding curtain. Johanna, Bibi's sister, slept in a little loft up a flight of stairs. It must be admitted, however, that there was some constraint to keep our bedtime activities at a discreet noise level. The stone and cement cottage did not exceed 600 square feet.

There was water and electricity but no bathroom facilities. A galvanized pail served as a toilet but I never mastered the ability to defecate suspended in air over that pail. I had to go into town to use a sit-down toilet. There also was no shower or bathtub. I, of course, used the shower on base all week but the family had to go to a public swimming pool about once a week to bathe. Iceland is a land of naturally heated thermal swimming pools. Swimming is the national sport. Every town has a pool, even those with populations of less than 200 souls. There were about half-a-dozen pools in the Reykjavic area. When I visited one, I realized that it also served as social club where old friends percolated together regularly in a relaxed atmosphere. These descendents of the Vikings swim outdoors even in the depth of winter. The temperature of the water ranges from 90 degrees to 110 degrees Fahrenheit.

Alongside the house was a plot of land that was used to grow potatoes. I volunteered to help Johanna clear the stones in preparation for the spring planting. I worked with her steadily but the earth seemed to be gaining on us, pushing up more stones to be discovered as fast as we removed the existing ones. After three hours, I, the young, well-fed soldier, was pooped and quit, but Johanna, a tough, lanky woman in her thirties, continued to shovel, bend and haul for another three hours. As far as I could see, her main source of nourishment and energy was coffee and cigarettes. Her boyfriend or husband was a fisherman and was away at sea for long periods. When he did return after a couple of months, I was thrilled because the first thing he did was build a sit-down outhouse on the front porch.

One day I went grocery shopping in Hafnarfjordur to replenish food supplies at the house. It was a one-man grocery store. As I checked out, the owner asked me a question in English to which I responded in Icelandic. He blinked. He was floored. Our conversation expanded. He thought perhaps I was a *vesturislandingur*. This term, western Icelander, was used to describe members of the sizeable colony of Icelanders who emigrated early in the century and settled in west Canada around Halifax. He generously suggested I share dinner with his family later in the week.

Now that I had started to meld into the Icelandic populace I decided to melt more subtly into the scenery and decided to replace my military uniform with common civilian clothing while I was off base, at least in less visible areas like Hafnarfjordur. Bibi's house was just off the Keflavik-Reykjavik

The Heart is a Funny Reservoir

road but was situated in a depression that effectively hid it from view from the road. Dinner at my grocer friend's house was an interesting experience for a couple of reasons. The family consisted of the man and his wife, a daughter of about 12 and a 17-year-old son. As we sat around the table in the small dining room I immediately noticed that only four places had been set. And when the dinner started it was clear that the mother was going to serve the dinner but was not going to eat with us. She would disappear into the kitchen after each course. I, of course, objected, but she smilingly refused to join us. Even in Syrian society, where females are not as highly valued as males, I had not seen such an overt demonstration of sexism. SY women served and SY men were served but the women always had a place at the dinner table. She served a meal of soup, boiled fish and potatoes and pudding which was simple but digestible.

The other interesting matter was that the son, Olaf, had four riding horses. I had always liked horseback riding and I rode frequently in Brooklyn. Ocean Parkway had five miles of bridal trails that continued to curl through Prospect Park, the park where Elba and I were first deflowered. Hemstead, Long Island, also had great trails and once Nate Dweck and I got the ultimate machismo high there by riding at a fast trot for two hours in a driving sleet storm.

Foreigners refer to the Icelandic horse as a pony because of the relatively diminutive size. They stand 13 "hands" high compared to a full-size horse of 15 or 16 "hands." They are not ponies. These horses are unique since they have not been crossbred since their importation by the Norsemen over 1000 years ago. It is against the law to import any other breed of horse into the island. They are beautiful, gentle animals and surprisingly strong. Olaf and I went riding. There were several unusual things about riding an Icelandic horse. First of all, you cannot post the trot as you do with a regular horse which permits you to rise and fall in rhythm with the horse's motion. The Icelandic horse's legs are so short and fast moving that there is no time for posting and you have to sit in the saddle and take the blows. There is also a singular gait called the *tolt* where the horse moves at a fast pace and you sit back and float along smoothly. We groomed our horses, saddled them and mounted. "You wanna race?" I looked out at the lava field stretching before us, strewn with gravel, rocks and boulders and thought this Olaf kid must be nuts for wanting to race. We were sure to get thrown at the first stumble. So I answered, "Sure!" And off we took. At full speed these horses had an uncanny ability to pick their way through the obstacles with nary a trip. I always lost the races because I tried to maintain a scintilla of sanity and held my horse back a bit.

Bibi and I used our weekends to avail ourselves of the recreational activities offered by Reykjavik. We sampled the restaurants, the few nightspots, dances, and movies. The days grew gradually longer and lighter. Spring had now arrived and Bibi suggested that we go visit her brother who lived on a small farm in the western fjords about 120 miles north of Reykavik. I arranged to take a week-long leave and prepared to plunge into the outback of Icelandic civilization.

Chapter Six
FURLOUGH TIME

The name Reykjavik means "smoky bay" which the original settlers used, undoubtedly, to refer to the steam escaping from subterranean streams in the area. Bibi and I drove through Hafnarfjordur and then Reykjavik in a heavy early morning fog. She was looking forward to visiting her brother whom she had not seen for a year and I was looking forward to touring half the country with a friendly native guide at my side. Bibi was not erudite, but she was typically energetic and cheerful. We chattered on about trifles. As we left the city behind and headed north, the sun rose on our right and drank up the mist, smiling brightly on our path. It also highlighted the reality that our road from here on would be more serpentine and serrated than the road from Keflavik.

Our first stop was Hvalafjord, so named because it was a whaling station. As we drove down to the shore we heard the whining winches and then saw a massive, shiny black carcass being hauled up a long concrete ramp which ran down to the sea. In the small bay another whale was tethered to a fishing vessel. The whale on the ramp was shorn of its flippers and tail and then by being rotated was stripped of its skin and blubber. There was a modest-sized rendering plant on site that extracted the whale oil by heat. I was informed that this was a Minke whale, one of 75 different whale species. One full-grown male Minke could provide up to 2000 pounds of meat and blubber. Whales are mammals; they bleed like mammals and the scene before us was gory. But then beef and lamb slaughter houses are certainly no less bloody and most people don't give it a thought as they sear, season, slice and swallow the results.

Bibi met a distant cousin working on the dock. In an in-breeding country as small as Iceland, there are very few degrees of separation from one person to another. Relatives are everywhere. He told us that he had also been whaling in the Faroe Islands and described how they use a line of boats to stampede a school of whales toward the shore where they get beached on the rocks or are otherwise trapped in shallow water. The whole town comes down to share in the sanguinary harvest.

Whaling station at Hvalafjord

On the way to Bogarnes, our next stop, we parked the car several times to take hikes into the countryside. Bogarnes was a town of a few hundred people with a couple of small inns. The inn we chose was on a slight rise over the town which gave us a vista of the whole town clinging to the edge of the long bay leading out to the Atlantic. We took advantage of our rest stop to relax in the hot waters of the Borgarnes swimming pool before having dinner. We barely succeeded in getting through dinner without nodding off to sleep.

We drove on northward through the sparsely populated land. The early summer landscape of green fields flowing around the outcroppings of rocks and stretching to black craggy mountains where melting glacial ice fed rainbow-hued misty waterfalls overwhelmed the eyes and tingled the spirit. Following Bibi's directions to her brother's farm, we turned west off the main road on a trail that meandered out to the far reaches of the fjords. I noticed that eight-foot long whale ribs had been planted at intervals along the path. These were being used to mark the trail during the winters when the land in this area cowered under a very deep blanket of snow. I wondered how these hardy people coped with the utter loneliness of the land, particularly in the night-dark winters. The countryside can be majestic, with breathtaking landscapes, but the humans clinging to life here are tiny and fragile beings facing the cruel indifference of nature.

Gunnar and his wife welcomed us with smiles and hugs. Their small abode looked like a combination house and barn because that was what it was. There were four cows in the barn adjoining the kitchen which added a certain warmth and fragrance to the ambience. It was also convenient. As we were sitting down to dinner, the wife stooped through the small connecting doorway and in a few minutes was back with an earthenware pitcher of warm freshly squeezed milk.

The farm hosted about one hundred sheep and a couple of sheep dogs. The fenced-in fields were emerald green, brighter than the dark blue ocean in the near distance, but a softly rich backdrop for the moving splotches of grazing white forms. With a shouted command from Gunnar, the dogs raced to round up the sheep and deftly moved them from one field to the other. Not a straggler was neglected. I marveled not only at their skill but also at how well the dogs understood Icelandic.

There wasn't sufficient room to accommodate Bibi and me in the house, and since we declined to reenact a Joseph and Mary in the barn with the cows, Gunnar set up a tent for us in front of the house. He milked the situation for all its comic effect.

"We're sorry that you two will have to sleep in the tent."

"Oh, that's perfectly OK. We'll manage."

"There's no heat out there. Do you think you'll be able to keep each other warm?"

"We'll do what we can."

"Oh, we forgot to tell you about the sleeping bags. We had two, but lent one to a cousin, so you two will have to share one one-person sleeping bag."

"Well I don't know about that."

"And would you mind sharing the tent with the dogs? They aren't very big."

"The dogs?!"

Now, Icelandic people have never heard of king- or queen-size beds. The bed I shared with Bibi at her house was no more than 36 inches wide and I never saw any other in the country wider than that. It's what you'd call a "cozy" size for two people. But sharing a one-person sleeping bag, I thought, was pushing that type of envelope too far. Gunnar, of course, just happened, at the last minute, to find the second sleeping bag and informed us that the dogs had requested to be allowed to sleep outside the tent. Sleeping in the fresh fjord air was invigorating and we did share one sleeping bag – for a while. I felt sad about the dogs, though.

An early morning breakfast was accompanied by all sorts of good-natured innuendos about how we had survived the night. We all beamed, embraced and said goodbye. The dogs wagged their tails.

Akureyri is the second-largest Icelandic city after Reykjavik. It is situated in the middle of the northern coast of the island at the base of a long scenic fjord. The twin-spired Lutheran church erected on a hill in the center of the city is a well-known landmark that we could see as we approached the city from afar.

An unfortunate incident, however, had marred the trip from the farm to the city. As one drives the dirt roads through the countryside, flocks of sheep graze the fields bordering the road and, at times, some of them will be ambling along the road itself. As a car approaches, the sheep on the road will scatter off to each side. I was driving at about 45 miles per hour. In front of us was a large flock of sheep and they started to scatter. Suddenly one of the lambs that had darted to the right, thinking perhaps that its mother was on the other side of the road, reversed course and raced back in front of the car. It died instantly. I stopped a few yards down the road and we got out of the car. Bibi started to cry and I held her close to my chest as we looked at the mangled little body. I had a painful sense of guilt that I knew would stay with me. If only I had been driving more slowly. If only I had reacted more quickly. If only.

A room at the largest hotel in Akureyri had been reserved but even so the room was furnished with two 24-inch-wide beds. We arrived late but as the daylight hours were stretching out toward midnight, particularly here in the north of Iceland, we found that an outdoor festival was in full voice. There was music to dance and sing to and snacks like fiskibrot for sale. The experience of dancing in the streets at midnight near the Arctic Circle engraved an indelible memory. We finally got to our narrow beds about four a.m. after a full day of travel and a full night of revelry.

Things between Bibi and me had been going smoothly up to now but taking vacations together puts any relationship to the test. The second day in Akureyri began ominously. Bibi was sulking. Evidently something I had done or said had offended her, but in my male obtuseness I shrugged it off as insignificant. That in itself was a grievous sin. By the time I got around to apologizing for I didn't know what, she had barricaded herself behind a wall of silence. Reconciliation, of course, was impossible as long as one party to the dispute refused to discuss the issue. At dinnertime – we ate at the hotel dining room – she was still angry, would not leave the room and refused to eat. I pleaded and reasoned and then stormed out slamming the door and went down to the dining room alone. It was sort of awkward eating alone when all the hotel personnel knew that I had come in with a female companion.

The 270-mile trip back to Reykjavik was mostly silent, but we decided to make a stop off at Thingvillir. All Icelanders know this location because the Althing or Parliament was established there over one thousand years ago. The hills sloping down to the stream were covered with a luxuriant thick grass. It became a playground for Bibi and me and thawed the frostiness between us. We chased each other. Back and forth we ran. When I caught her, I tackled her and clasped together we rolled down the hill laughing to the point of exhaustion. Finally, physically and emotionally relaxed, we fell asleep in a sheltered nook under the warm sun, protected by the ghosts of generations of Icelandic leaders. When we walked back to the car we held hands.

Chapter Seven
WE HAVE LOVED

My military colleagues on base were surprised to learn that I had wasted a whole week of my furlough time touring the island. At least, they thought it a waste. In fact, there were some who took a negative attitude toward my intermingling with Icelandics and the fact that I spoke the language made me downright subversive. My section chief, Captain Gullekson, obliquely criticized me for it and even said he had heard reports that I had been wearing civilian clothes in town. Although I was punctual and efficient in my work at the main headquarters, he soon exiled me to a small warehouse on the outskirts of the camp. I was not displeased. It was peaceful there. With the assistance of one private, I handled and recorded the inflow and outflow of specialized base supplies. I was also one step removed from direct supervision by the captain since I now reported to a new, timid second lieutenant named Parsons.

My roommate Sergeant Dixon had been repatriated. He had always hassled me about my choice of music in our room. A monthly record of classical music arrived for me every month from the Musical Heritage Society, but Dixon much preferred what could be called shit-kickin' music. Beethoven and Bach were tough enough for him but Boris Goudounov drove him out of the room. There was less hassle with his replacement Corporal Kowalski since I outranked him. My friend Private Henderson was promoted to private first class because of his meritorious service in spit shining his boots. He had joined the army chorus on base and the concerts they presented periodically were really quite good. I asked him if he would be interested in an Icelandic blind date but he demurred. Corporal Madden continued to carry himself with a stiff beatific air while still being pursued by his private alcoholic demon. You could have sliced bread with the starched creases of his uniform. He winked at me with pleasure when I complimented his sharper image. Alcoholism is no stranger to Iceland and examples of it were evident to me in Reykjavik.

The reliable Chevrolet had taken a beating on the week-long trip around the island and a couple of parts in the suspension system had broken. The car was my physical link to the world off base. There was no Chevy dealership with service and parts departments located in Iceland. But there was a blacksmith in Keflavik. A better name for this craftsman would have been metalworks sculptor. He was able to recreate or repair just about any part for any car with his hammer, anvil and blowtorch. The car was back in serviceable condition in a few hours. If things got bad enough mechanically, he could always outfit you with shoes for your horse.

The activities on base continued on their daily routine except for the newly instituted weekly march. The base commander thought that we would be in better fighting shape if we, predominately office-based soldiers, went for a promenade once week for an hour or so. Since it contributed to the national defense of our country, we considered it our patriotic duty to participate.

There was also a flurry of activity when word was passed down the chain of command that a two-star general would be paying a visit to the base in three weeks. Special requisitions were issued to replace or repair all the base equipment. Everything paintable was painted, including curbstones and flower garden borders in the most remote corners of the camp. Floors were waxed and streets swept. Vehicles were washed and lubricated. Uniforms were spotless and boots gleamed. Everything was pristine when G-day arrived. The general landed at noon, was taken directly to the officers' club where he had a few drinks, smoked a cigar and was served a lunch of boeuf bourguignonne with pearl onions. He was then returned to his plane and took off at 2:30 p.m. We had evidently passed inspection.

The general had no knowledge of what the commoners' life on the base was like and even less knowledge of the life that pulsed around us outside the base. Bibi had a friend named Gudrun. Gudrun had had an American boyfriend, but as she had grown into the sixth month of her pregnancy he had grown more and more distant until he was barely a speck on the horizon. We took her with us occasionally to a nightspot or a dance. One Saturday in early June when I arrived from the base in the late afternoon, Bibi said that she and Gudrun would be going out visiting after dinner but they would be back shortly. We supped and they took off. It was still daylight so I looked up my horsy buddy, wild Olaf, but I found out he and some friends were gone on a week-long horseback riding trek up north. I went back to the house, did some weeding in the potato garden, read my book and waited. And waited. Johanna was at the house, her man having again gone down to the sea in ships. She was sitting in the kitchen with her nourishing cigarette and coffee.

"Where could Bibi be? It's past 10 o'clock and she said she would be right back."

"Well…"

"Is it possible she missed the bus or maybe the busses don't run this late."

"Didn't she tell you where she was going?"

"No, she just said she was going visiting."

"I have to tell you she probably won't be back till late."

"Why? Where did she go?"

"She and Gudrun went to a dance."

"A dance! How do you know that?"

"She told me before she left."

I was stunned but more than stunned I was hurt. And then I was angry. At midnight, I pulled the curtains to block out the daylight and went to bed. About an hour later Bibi came in. She slid into bed beside me. Not a word passed between us. She knew I was awake. I turned away from her to face the wall. I didn't fall asleep. My mind did somersaults trying to figure out why she pulled such a dirty trick on me. On one of the somersaults I realized the upside of the situation. Perhaps this was the best of all situations. There were certain things about our relationship with which I was already dissatisfied. She worked as a part-time waitress which provided her with very little of interest to talk about. I never saw her read a book. She was moody. The woman didn't bathe often enough and you could tell. I had my justification or excuse. By the time the morning hours approached I had made up my mind that, regardless of her excuses or reasons, I would leave her.

"You lied to me, Bibi!"

"We didn't plan to stay out that late. The time just got away from us."

"But you said you were going to visit a friend but you didn't visit anybody. You went to a dance."

"We changed our mind. Gudrun said…"

"That's not true. You knew you were on your way to go dancing when you left the house. You left me alone last night and I'm leaving you now."

"No, you're not!"

I had packed my few things in my bag and when I turned to leave she had thrust her back against the door with her arms outstretched. I tried to brush her aside but was astounded at the violence of her resistance. She fought me bitterly, blocking the door with all her strength. Tears streamed down her face and she pleaded. I was adamant. I had never in my life beaten a woman but we stood there, face to face, body to body, will to will, panting in an agonizing confrontation. Suddenly I whirled and flung my travel bag through a small window on the other side of the room. Without a thought of image or pride, I crawled out that same window and made my escape.

Most Icelanders will not deny the existence of fairies, elves or ghosts. These ephemeral beings live or hover in enchanted places called *alagabettir* which are all over the country. Even construction engineers here will avoid disturbing such places and their supernatural inhabitants. As I drove away from Hafnarfjordur a strange apparition filled my mind. My harsh break with Bibi had left a sad emptiness now inside me. I was alone again yet still yearning for an emotional fulfillment. It brought up the image of an Icelandic fairy I had known only fleetingly but whose magic had stayed with me in the reservoir of my memory. I would search for the enchanted place and that fairy. I would try to find Ragnheider Ingvarsdottir.

Chapter Eight
A BEAUTIFUL AUBURN-HAIRED NURSE

"Professor Thorlafson, I have a problem."
"Icelandic vocabulary or grammar?"
"Neither, thanks. I'm trying to find someone and I don't have any idea how to go about it."
"Who is this person?"
"It's an Icelandic woman that I met about six months ago. Since then I've seen her and chatted briefly with her about two or three times. I would like to see her again if I can, but as soon as possible."
"Well, Iceland has a pretty small population and Reykjavik has about half of the country's people. What do you know about her? Does she live in Reykjavik?"
"Yes, she lives in Reykjavik. Her name is Ragnheider Ingvarsdottir and all I know about her is that she works as a nurse, where, I can't remember."
"How old is she?"
"Oh, I guess about my age. In her early twenties."
"You know, Icelanders are like one big family and I have lived in Reykjavik all my life. I think I can help you. I should be able to locate her in a couple of days."
When he came out to the base that week to give Mac and me our weekly language lesson, Mr. Thorlafson handed me a slip of paper with a number on it. It was the phone number of the clinic where Ragnheider worked. Mac, who knew about my quest, gave me a thumbs up. The next day, when I dialed the number, my heart was racing as if this were the first date of my life. I asked for Ragnheider and after a long, long minute she picked up the phone.
"Dottie, I don't know if you remember me. I'm Ed, the American sergeant from Keflavik."
"Ed?"

"Ah...yes. *Hinn hermadur sem tala islensku?* The soldier that speaks Icelandic?"

"Oh, that Ed! Yes, Eddie, of course I remember you! How many soldiers speak even bad Icelandic? And you're that great dancer."

"Well, I hope my dancing is better than my Icelandic."

"They're both better than average. It's wonderful to hear from you."

"It's more than wonderful to hear you say that."

Reykjavik was not the most beautiful capital in the world, but it did have a cleanliness and brightness in summer that was unique. And with less than 100,000 residents it was probably one of the most manageable capitals for an outsider. There was no sense of tension typical of big city hustle and bustle. Lined with trees, Lake Tjornin, in the center of town, harbored a variety of cacophonous seabirds. The lakeside benches also beckoned to a variety of cooing lovebirds. It was here that Dottie and I were to meet for our first date.

During the week, American soldiers were permitted to leave the base after the workday ended at 5 p.m. but were required to be back on base before the midnight curfew. On the weekends, we were off from noon on Saturday until midnight Sunday. Special duty assignments could cut into your after-hour free time but in the supply arm of the service that was infrequent. I had been in the habit of spending one weekday evening and the weekend in town.

It was a Wednesday evening about 7 p.m. that Dottie and I started to get acquainted. Neither of us was presumptuous, we didn't rush things, we were simply polite and friendly. We both had had dinner since her workday also ended at 5 p.m. We sat chatting by the sun-reflecting silver lake for a while and then she took me for a tour of the city. She showed me the granite Parliament House and I couldn't help but recall how Bibi and I had romped on the fields of Thingvillir where the Parliament had been located for almost a thousand years until this lava stone building in front of us was built in 1881. We passed by the National Theatre which had placards posted attesting to an active program of concerts, operas and other events. In addition to home-grown talent, there were regular presentations by visiting artists from overseas. She claimed that the Icelandic Symphony was well thought of and went on international tours. Dottie pointed out several bookstores, noting that Iceland has more bookstores per capita and publishes more books per capita than the United States. An author I had never heard of, named Halldor Laxness, had just been awarded the Nobel Prize for literature which seemed an incredible feat for someone writing in Icelandic. His works, of course, had been translated into other languages.

We eventually ended up at a coffee shop/restaurant where we ran into a group of her friends. Since I was not wrestling rocks or riding horses in Hafnarfjordur, I was in full military dress. Her friends started talking through me as if I were a deaf mute until Dottie warned them that I understood Icelandic. It was a practice she was to repeat many times. My presence as a sentient being was thereby acknowledged and the atmosphere around me became amiable. Before I returned to camp, Dottie showed me the clinic where she worked and then we walked the six or seven blocks to where her apartment was located. It was a walk-up four-story house. Dottie lived on the fourth floor with her sister Lolly, each having a small bedroom with the invariable narrow bed and sharing a bathroom in the hallway which contained a toilet and a sink. She parried my questioning look by saying that she was able to shower every workday at the clinic. There was a third bedroom on the floor occupied by an old man whom I rarely saw. I reflected that the repeated four-flight climb would either contribute to his longevity or soon do him in.

It was time to return to base. We were to rendezvous again on Saturday night. The regular Saturday night dance was scheduled but there would be a house party given by one of Dottie's girlfriends before the dance. Evidently this was a normal Icelandic custom, having a small party before going on to a bigger party. In the course of our conversation, Dottie revealed that she had been going with an Air Force lieutenant for several months but that they had broken off the relationship about a month before my call. I chose not to probe further on this subject. I started to tell her about the situation concerning Bibi but she surprised me. She probably knew more about Bibi and her past than I did. She was also cognizant of the beginning and end of our affair. She smiled enigmatically and I shook my head. If nothing else, this present timing of our friendship had been serendipitous.

We had had an enjoyable and educational evening together. It was past eleven o'clock but the June sky was still as light blue as her eyes. We said goodbye in front of her building, which was where I would pick her up Saturday. We kissed once lightly, sweetly. I drove away on a cloud and didn't feel any of the thumps on the winding dirt road back to the Keflavik Air Force Base.

Chapter Nine
ONE BRIEF SUMMER

Dottie and her sister Lolly were waiting outside the house when I arrived on Saturday night. They didn't look like sisters. Where Dottie had a warm reddish tint to her complexion and hair, with a small sharp-edged nose and delicate features, Lolly was a statuesque Nordic blonde with bold classic features and full lips. I suspected that perhaps one or both were foster children raised by the same parents. This suspicion was misplaced, however, as they were, in fact, true siblings. We chatted in the evening breeze as we waited for Lolly's boyfriend.

When he turned the corner and approached I had to smile because I already knew him slightly, although I didn't realize he had an Icelandic girlfriend. Corporal Demerjian was dark-haired and good looking. He was one of the soldiers that was involved in the contraband trade, buying goods from the post exchange (PX) and selling them to the Icelandics. Consequently, I saw him frequently in town making his rounds. He had told me once about how much money he made buying diamond engagement rings for resale. Diamonds were his best friends because they were so valuable, portable and concealable. The merchandise at the PX was exempt from import duties and other sales taxes which was not the case for goods imported and sold through normal Icelandic commercial channels. The personnel at the PX must have wondered at the frivolity of Demerjian's love life considering all the engagement rings that he had bought. Interestingly enough, he had presented one of the rings to Lolly. He declared that he was arranging to take her back to the States with him and they would be married there.

I wondered what the attitude of Icelandic women was concerning marriage to American servicemen. Did they consider it an escape to an exciting Hollywoodian world of fancy clothes, big cars and suburban homes? Were they attracted by colorful states like California and big cities like New

York? How would they react to being uprooted from the insular homogenous culture and language to which they were accustomed? There are pluses and minuses in all life decisions but where did love fit into this equation? Did two people from widely different backgrounds have any hope for a long-term successful relationship? All these profound perplexities of the future were swept aside by the force of the Now that carried us forward to tonight's party.

Dottie's girlfriend lived in a modern twelve-story apartment building. The festivities were underway when we arrived. About two dozen people milled around, drinking, smoking, talking. Two couples were dancing to the music from the phonograph where His Master's Voice was pouring out a polyglot profusion of songs. Riffling through the records, I was amused to see one with the Andrew Sisters singing my old bittersweet favorite from the days of the national strike, "Mr. Sandman, Send Me a Dream." I put it on and Dottie and I started dancing. She nestled her head on my shoulder and we continued dancing, our bodies becoming more and more closely pressed together.

After an hour or so, Dottie went up to her friend and whispered something to which the friend quickly nodded assent. She came back to me, took my hand and we followed the hostess to one of the two bedrooms in the apartment. The door was opened, we entered and the door closed behind us. A dim lamp glowed on the bedside table. The not-so-narrow bed had a huge fluffy quilt on it and Dottie kicked off her shoes and climbed up. She lay back and stretched out her arms to me. I was, of course, eager, ready and appreciative of the liberal national morals that permitted something like this to happen so naturally, but two things troubled me. First of all, should I stay in uniform? I could de-uniform in fairly short order but the combat boots were particularly time consuming to unlace and then to re-lace. Secondly, there was still a noisy party taking place on the other side of the bedroom door. What happened if someone opened the door? With military bravura, I decided to go all the way, although I did keep on my underwear, just in case. She opened herself to me and enfolded me. I had been to many parties in my life but none with such scintillating refreshments.

When we returned to the living room we found that Lolly and Dermerjian had gone on to the dance along with half of the convivial crowd. They hadn't thought to disturb us when the hostess told them where we were. Dottie and I were feeling very comfortable together. I didn't have the feeling that I had had frequently in the past after having sex; a feeling that now that the hunger was assuaged, I would just as soon retreat into my own private space until the hunger arose again. With Dottie, I preferred staying in her presence, linking arms and gliding with her, going on to the ball, a prince who had just found his Cinderella again. And she was my Icelandic passport. We found the others and danced till two in the morning or perhaps it was till two in the afternoon. They both looked about the same and I had lost track of time.

"That was a fancy tango you just did, Dottie. Have I exhausted you yet?"

"Absolutely, I'm absolutely exhausted and absolutely happy."

"I'm happy too. Listen, I know we haven't discussed what happens after the dance. Shall I drop you off home and go back to the base?"

"Absolutely not!"

"You're so absolutely absolute tonight."

"You are so right and I will be absolutely insulted if you don't accept my hospitality tonight, particularly after I went and got you a gift."

"A gift? What kind of a gift could you possibly get me?"

"A gift that will please an Icelandic nut like you."

In her room she handed me a brightly wrapped packet which turned out to contain an Icelandic folk song book with lyrics for about a hundred songs. Even though it was late, we stayed up, scrunched on her damn narrow bed, as she taught me in her mezzo voice two of her favorites. After a couple of run-throughs, I was able to do a credible job of holding up my end of the duet. I fell asleep on my side with the melodies and lyrics circling my brain.

Shafts of fiery light slipped through the gaps in the heavy window curtains and I awoke the next morning with a kink in my side and a crick in my neck. A narrow bed for two may be nice for certain activities but sleeping isn't one of them. In addition to the paucity of space for two flat-on-the-back sleepers, every motion of one person prevents the other from falling into a deep slumber. I arose stiffly and went to the bathroom and on my way back I saw Dermerjian sleepily stumble out of Lolly's room. We barely nodded to each other saying not a word. Lolly was a considerably bigger woman than Dottie and I mused as to how much sleeping space was left for Dermerjian.

Sunday was indeed sunny with a perfectly clear sky and the omnipresent wind, brisk and sea-scented. The day before we had picked up tickets at the National Theatre for a Sunday matinee ballet performance by a visiting Danish troupe. We had a tough lunch of mutton stew, at least tough for a guy like me raised by a doting mother on baby loin lamb chops. I had also been raised on Ballanchine's New York City Ballet and I found the Danish troupe, although a pleasant respite, a couple of rungs below the talent of the Ballanchine company. I, of course, said nothing of the kind to Ragnheider.

After the performance we returned to her home base and we hung out, reading, practicing our Icelandic song repertoire and making love. Dottie had already begun to smooth out my discordant edges not only in my music making but also in my lovemaking. When I made a move to get out of bed immediately after our lovemaking to go to the bathroom to discard the condom and wash up, she ordered me to stay put and to hold her in a soft embrace. Her auburn hair was spread Medusa-like on the white pillow, subtly complemented by her rouged lips and the areolas of her breasts. It was a very convincing argument and as a good soldier I followed her orders.

And that is how I discovered the pleasures of sexual afterglow.

Our first weekend together was over. If the Army could guarantee me weekends like this all year long, I would be ready to reenlist.

Chapter Ten
LINGUISTICALLY COMPATIBLE

"You know, Dottie, I'm so sad that I'm so glad to be in your pad now."

"I don't think my English is good enough to understand what you're talking about."

"Well, let me explain it so that your Icelandic mind can grasp it. Six months ago I was out fishing. And there you were, a beautiful, bright-eyed, silvery codfish swimming within reach of my net. And if I had only made an extra effort at that moment and spread my net I might have caught that attractive fish. And I would have been feasting since then."

"So you think I remind you of a codfish?"

"That's not the point. The point is I think you're a very classy codfish and I regret the fact that instead of two weeks I could have been enjoying your company for six months."

"You can make believe that I'm the first Icelandic girl you have met."

"OK and you can make believe that I'm the first American boy you have met."

"As you Americans say 'it's a deal.'"

The linguistic divide between Dottie and me was not too broad to leap, although at times it required a mix of both languages to avoid falling into a chasm of misunderstanding. Mr. Thorlofsson had provided Mac and me with an Icelandic book combining grammar, reading selections and a glossary. The impetus for writing the book in 1942 was the launching of Icelandic courses at John Hopkins University designed for American officers assigned to Iceland. There never was much interest and the courses didn't get off the ground but the very complete and excellent textbook by Stefan Einarsson did get published. Book learning has its place in conquering a new language but it receives an invaluable boost by immersion in the milieu in which it is spoken. Speaking sweet somethings to a girlfriend like Ragnheider and hearing her responses in that tongue also contributed to my motivation and progress. I could tell, of course, that Dottie had an advantage over me because she had had many more contacts with Americans over the years than I had had with Icelandics.

All languages evolve, certain words die out, meanings change, new words enter, sometimes created out of native roots, sometimes borrowed from other languages. English, for example, has many words from Latin, the mother language of Spanish, but there also have been many relatively recent borrowings of Spanish words into English and English words into Spanish. Consequently, English and Spanish share thousands of cognates. The Old Norse Icelandic language, however, did not follow a normal linguistic evolution. Due to its isolation as a remote island, foreign influences on its language were minimal. In addition, the early tradition of written sagas known to all served to stabilize the language in much the way the Bible preserved Hebrew. An Icelandic youth could read a 900-year-old saga today and understand it without difficulty. I could not do the same thing with Old English. The small size of the population and its mobility within this small country precluded regional dialects. Language reflects its people. It appeared to me that Icelanders had proudly maintained the purity of their language and refused to incorporate foreign words into its vocabulary. I could read through a whole page of an Icelandic newspaper and not find one English cognate. And English speakers found it a nightmare to pronounce. Sure it was harder to sing but still I sang.

The Icelandic songbook Dottie had given me was also a great language learning aid. The mind is a funny archive. If you once learn well a series of words attached to a melody it will stick with you for decades. And sentiments expressed in songs in some way have the ring of truth about them. A sampling of songs that Dottie taught me included a sad lilting waltz about Hilda. Young, rosy Hilda fell in love and her lover goes to sea and the song advises "spin, spin my Hilda/he will soon return to you" but finally acknowledges "Hilda spun and spun/And her heart burned up/Never did her lover return." Another is a stirring riding song where the horseman exults in the galloping speed and strength of his horse and the feel of the wind in his face. A third song, that was my favorite, concerned an expatriate who asks a thrush migrating back to Iceland to carry his love for his country and girl with him.

It was the week of the summer solstice. There was no midnight sun in Reykjavik but it came close. The sun would dip below the horizon for about an hour. Sunset and sunrise almost ran into each other. It was at this time that

Dottie threw a new number into our love equation. She informed me that she was going up north for a week to spend some time with her three-year-old son. Her son! Evidently her son was being raised by her parents in her hometown. I was caught a bit off balance but of course agreed that it was something that she had to do.

The weekend before her departure we kept up a steady stream of activities ostensibly avoiding focusing on the history of her son. We walked, we danced, we sang but we knew that a new dimension had been added to our relationship. We even took a trip a couple of hours outside of Reykjavik to visit a forest called Vaglaskogue.

In mufti in Vaglaskogue forest

Iceland basically is a treeless country although there is strong evidence that it was once fairly heavily forested along the coasts. Deforestation by settlers also damaged the land by depriving it of the protection from erosion afforded by tree roots. The country was trying to repair the damage by controlled planting programs. The progress was slow – unlike beanstalks, trees don't grow overnight. The forest that Dottie took me to probably had about 100 trees and those trees were not very tall, topping out at about 12 feet. I understood it was a very serious crime to destroy a tree in Iceland. It was pleasant to roam through this untypical Icelandic terrain on a bright day. I started to fantasize privately about taking a trip together with Dottie to Europe. I wanted to work out some of the practical details first before I broached the subject to her. For Dottie it would have been pure fantasy because she had never before left the island.

Chapter Eleven
SCOTLAND AND ENGLAND

    The Keflavik Air Force Base had more or less regular military flights from Iceland to the United Kingdom, generally to the Prestwick airport near Glasglow, Scotland. Depending upon seat availability, military personnel were allowed to fly free of charge. The Icelandic airline also flew to Prestwick from Reykjavik with regular scheduled flights. As Dottie and I fleshed out our plans for our continental vacation, I suggested that I would take the military flight, she would take the commercial flight and we would meet at Prestwick. Since it was understood that I was paying for the whole trip it would logically be my call. I sensed her insecurity with this arrangement – what if the military flight didn't materialize – so I decided we would fly together commercially.

    I had two weeks furlough accumulated and Dottie could only take a week off at this time since she had been gone a week to visit her child. She called a couple days before our departure with the discouraging news that she was sick but then she clarified it by the fact that she would only be "calling in sick" in order to take off the first day of our vacation. The plan was to spend a week together in England, after which, she would return to Reykjavik and I would go on to a U.S. Army rest and recreation center at Garmisch-Partikirken in the Bavarian Alps for four or five days before returning.

    Our flight from Reykjavik left early in the morning so I slept overnight at Dottie's apartment. Neither of us slept much due to the pre-flight excitement. We arrived in Glasgow around noon and found an inn surrounded by a flowered garden. After a lunch of lamb stew we fell into the lumpy but large bed for a siesta. That evening we roamed Glasgow finding it a rather drab city. The nearby countryside was lovely, however, and we planned to spend part of the next day floating on the oft sung about Loch Lomond. It turned out an unusually perfect day for us because in addition to a cloudless sky, there was no wind. Icelanders like us expected wind every day. Row boats were available for rent and soon we were gliding tranquilly over the glassy water. Dottie felt so gloriously relaxed that she removed her blouse and bra, closed her eyes and lay back in the prow of the boat as I, in the bow, continued to paddle, enjoying the scenery. Back in Glasgow, we fish and chipped away the rest of the day and caught the plane for the one-hour flight to London.

I had reserved a room for us at the Royal Park Hotel. I sweated it out when we entered the proper and sumptuous lobby and walked up the reception desk because I had registered under the name of Mr. and Mrs. Chalom. The clerk, however, insisted on seeing both our passports. Ingvarsdottir doesn't look much like Chalom, but the gentleman, in his clipped British tone, said that everything was in order for our arrival. It was a marvelous room overlooking the park and proffering a Queen Mary-size bed and a bathtub that would have floated a ship. After partaking of the warm waterworks, we leaped into bed.

"Eddie, *elsku min,* when you make love to me why don't you talk to me? Why don't you say, 'Dottie, you're sweet. Dottie, I love you'? Why don't you make love to all of me?"

I might have said that it was because I was ignorant and didn't understand much about a woman's sexual satisfaction. I might have said it was because I was too focused on my own orgasm to the exclusion of everything else. I might have said several things but all I did was mumble an indistinct apology. Dottie had once again shown me how to fine tune the harmony of love. She then added that I needn't interrupt the flow of events by putting on a contraceptive because she was sure that she could not get pregnant again. I agreed to her suggestion.

London was a ball. The first night we went to see Margot Fonteyn and the Royal Ballet in a performance of Swan Lake. We could only get standing room at the back of the auditorium. When the curtain arose, the combination of the Tchaikovsy music and exquisite dancing immediately brought tears to our eyes. We stood for two hours to watch the spectacular show but at least we didn't have to do it on our toes. England is not known for its cuisine but it does make accessible a wide variety of international restaurants. Indian, Chinese, French – we sampled them all. One afternoon Ragnheider took off by herself to do some department store shopping. She had brought her own limited funds for this purpose and I chipped in an extra twenty-five dollars. Soldiers didn't earn a heck of a lot of money but what I earned was quite a bit more than her salary and after she left I felt rotten that I had skimped on her. But even so, she returned thrilled with the clothes and accessories she had

The Heart is a Funny Reservoir

found. The rest of the time spent in London was active. We visited all the tourist attractions like the changing of the guard, the Tower of London, the wax museum and the art museums and we treasured the moments strolling through Hyde Park.

Our flights left London the same day, she going back to Iceland, I going on to Germany. The Second World War had been over for ten years but my feeling towards the Germans was ambivalent. In my stopover in Hamburg, the bombed-out ruins stood silent witness to horrors of the war from the destruction caused by the Allied bombing. As a youngster I had kept a scrapbook entitled "Lest We Forget" which described Nazi atrocities, and I wondered what role in this chilling drama had been played by each German I passed in the street now.

Garmisch-Partikirken was picture-postcard perfect and, as an Army R&R resort, it cost me nothing. The hotel was planted at the foot of the Zugspitze, the highest mountain in the Bavarian Alps. My first morning I went out for a walk about 8 a.m. and ran into two 17-year-old German students who were on vacation. During summer school vacations many students simple loaded their bicycles on trains and, at reduced rates, traveled to the scenic areas of the country. These two had come down from the north to climb the Zugspitze and invited me to join them. With reminiscences of my wild horseback rides with Olaf raising red flags, I said "sure." I already had my boots on, so how bad could it be?

The first four hours were only moderately difficult. We stopped to rest and my companions generously shared their lunch sandwiches with me. I had studied three years of German in high school and both students had studied English and were eager to practice on me, so again I found linguistic compatibility. The second half of the climb became increasingly steep and more challenging. Several times I considered giving up and turning back but my nationalistic or religious competitiveness would not let me. I would be dammed if I let these Germans beat me. So I struggled on. We reached the top about 5 p.m. Amazingly enough, there was a little chalet up there. The fact that one could choose to ride a cable car to the top for the view provided enough business for the chalet restaurant to survive. There were very few of the hardy like us that climbed the mountain on foot. We got some hot chocolate and apple strudel but we could not tarry. My friends pointed out that the light would fade soon and we would be climbing down the mountain mostly in the dark. Dark was an understatement. It was a moonless night and it became so black that the descent became a tactile adventure feeling our way down with my hand always on my buddy's shoulder. It was 3 a.m. before I said goodbye to my newfound friends at the hotel. We had been on that mountain for 19 hours.

At nine-thirty the next morning they came to call for me. They were on their way to climb the Zugspitze from the other side and wondered if I would like to join them. I arose stiffly and painfully from my bed and informed them that I would love to but that I, unfortunately, had a previous engagement. Later that morning I went to get a haircut and a massage.

The recreation part of the rest and recreation had been a success but Ragnheider Ingvarsdottir was waiting for me back in Reykjavik. I would be spending the last two days of my leave with her. I knew that her adept nurse's hands would resuscitate me physically and spiritually.

Chapter Twelve
DOTTIE AND I PARTED

I had been drafted in 1953, for a two-year tour of duty and so was due to be discharged in the November of 1955. A recent Army regulation, however, permitted early release under certain conditions. One of the conditions was that military personnel accepted into institutions of higher education with terms commencing in September and with less than ninety days left to serve in the Army were eligible for early release to start the fall term on time. I had applied to four universities and had been accepted by three of them. The one that lured me most strongly was the University of California at Los Angeles. It was only in late summer that I found out about the possibility of an early release from the Army and I promptly applied. My application was approved the first of September and I was to ship out to the States within a week.

I knew this would be a trying time for Dottie and me. We enjoyed each other's company and had been very close. Particularly close because we had traveled together overseas and we had shared many new and unique experiences. After my return from Germany, we continued our regular round of activities meeting once during the week and spending the entire weekend together. The summer was slipping by smoothly but we both knew it was bringing us closer to our final goodbye. Final goodbyes, as final as ours would be, are painful, but this regret was assuaged by the anticipation of my impending liberation from the regimentation of the military and the continuation of my college education. The opportunity to return to my previous employment was open to me. My ex-employers had been more than generous, continuing to send me commissions, while I was a soldier, on the sales to the accounts that I had opened for them. But I opted for wider vistas than selling infants wear.

It turned out that I had to practically fight my way out of the Army. There are many forms of discharge from military service. The three major categories are honorable, general and dishonorable. Honorable is the most common, but my section commander Captain Gullekson had recommended I receive a general discharge instead of an honorable one. The captain had never been comfortable with my independent attitude or my Icelandophile activities.

"Captain Gullekson, sir, I asked to see you so that you could explain to me why you had put me in for a general rather than an honorable discharge."

"Because that's what I think your performance is worth."

"But I've always fulfilled all my assignments and all my records are accurate and up to date."

"Well, Sergeant, we obviously have a difference of opinion and mine has more weight than yours."

"With all due respect, sir, you really don't know what work I've been doing. I report directly to Lieutenant Parsons and you personally never inspected my warehouse. I'm sure Lieutenant Parsons will back me up and confirm that I have always been on top of my job."

"If you can get Lieutenant Parsons to say that I'll change your rating."

"Lieutenant Parsons, Captain Gullekson gave me a poor rating on my job performance but you're here all the time and you know I've never had one complaint. He said that if you agree to say that I have done a good job he would change the rating."

"Sergeant Chalom, I know that you have done a good job but I can't tell the captain that."

"Why!?"

"He's so pissed off at you that even if I praised you it wouldn't make any difference to him."

"But that rating will affect the kind of discharge I get which may affect my GI Bill."

"That's tough. I'm sorry but I'm not going to get myself in bad with the captain. I've got too many months left to spend on this island."

The rating stood but somehow or other when my discharge papers were finalized it said "honorable" and I was enrolled in the educational benefits program of the GI Bill of Rights.

There were a few of us Icelandophiles on base but we were surrounded by a sea of Icelandophobes, guys who never looked on their enforced stay on the island as an opportunity to learn something new. Another fault line existed between draftees and regular Army soldiers. RAs looked on us draftees as men of a lesser god. There was one particular RA sergeant who had been heckling me for quite a while. He was particularly incensed at my friendships with Icelanders. I ignored or shrugged off his verbal abuse until my last day at the Keflavik base. All personnel being shipped back to the U.S. were gathered in a vacant barrack building awaiting the flight when this RA sergeant challenged me to a fight calling me a chicken-shit National Guard coward. It became quiet and everyone looked at us. I stood up and we walked toward each other down the center of the room like two gunfighters in a western film. He continued to spew out filthy epithets as we drew near and then he lunged for my throat. I knew some ju-jitsu and I quickly grabbed his left wrist with my right hand, pivoted halfway to the right swinging my left arm over and then under his left arm gripping my right wrist with my left hand and then jerking upward with all my strength. He went up in the air and crashed down on his back clasping his dislocated shoulder in pain. The fight had lasted about 30 seconds. I hoped that this altercation would not get me into an administrative mess that would delay my departure but the RA, out of good sportsmanship or shame, told the medics he had fallen down the stairs.

My other farewells were not quite as stressful or violent. I had bonded with my green 1952 Chevrolet during my tour on the island but now it was necessary for our paths to diverge. An agency of the Icelandic government purchased all cars left by the American military. There was no bargaining, they set a price which you had to accept. I actually received $100 more for the car than I had paid for it two years earlier so I had no complaint.

Professor Thorloffson, with his unfailing cigarette sprouting from his moustache, shook my hand. My colleague, smiling Mac, gave me a brotherly hug and promised he would carry on the good fight to overpower the Icelandic language. Private First Class Henderson was also taking advantage of the college early release program but was leaving on a later flight. He said he was glad to be graduating from the Army saying he had earned his release although he did not specify exactly how. My roommate Kowalski was probably relieved to see me pack up my classical records and move on. My alcoholic buddy Corporal Madden, standing erect, threw me a mock salute and wished me a good life. All these people had touched my life in Iceland and there was a touch of the bittersweet in saying goodbye. But none had touched my life as had Ragnheider Ingvarsdottir.

Dottie and I parted. It was inevitable, but inevitability whether in death or departure does not preclude heartache in spite of the fact that our liaison barely exceeded three months. I was 23 and I had not planned on entering the next phase of my youthful life encumbered with a wife and child. I felt that Dottie knew that this unspoken understanding had always shadowed our relationship. The beginning of our affair owed a lot to serendipitous timing; perhaps its ending was also a matter of timing. My mother knew absolutely nothing about my Icelandic girlfriends and undoubtedly was happier not knowing. It was not, either, that I had an attachment to my Brooklyn Syrian community with my hundreds of acquaintances and relatives living there. My military service and, especially my Icelandic adventure, had definitively severed that umbilical cord.

We passed our last weekend together but I hesitated from hour to hour to give Dottie the news about my imminent departure under the philosophy that the best pain is the shortest pain. We spent several hours outdoors in Reykjavik. The weather was typical, a partly sunny sky with scudding black clouds fleeing the inexorable winds. We took a long walk, had dinner followed by my favorite dessert of skyr at our regular restaurant and then went back to her apartment. It was only as I was ready to return to base that I broke the news that I would be leaving very shortly. My words came out haltingly, apologetically, but finally the deed was done. As I drove the road back to Keflavik for the last time, I experienced a polychromatic mixture of sentiments but I also guiltily breathed a sigh of relief.

Chapter Thirteen
48 YEARS

This memoir focuses on two brief periods in my life, the first in 1955 and the second in 2003. The 17,435 days in the intervening years is simply a footnote to the improbable story of Ragnheider Ingvarsdottir and her American lover that is presented in these pages. I fully expected that as I became immersed in the activities and relationships of my college life at UCLA the memories of my Icelandic sojourn would fade and disappear. I did receive a very moving letter from Ragnheider shortly after I left Iceland, a scarlet letter that branded itself on my brain. I sent a simple Christmas card from California in December and after that there was nothing but silence, a very long silence.

My ties with Iceland became tenuous. The first assignment I received as a new reporter for the UCLA *Daily Bruin* was a feature article on Haldor Laxness, the Icelander who had recently won the Nobel Prize for Literature. But apart from that, I met no Icelanders, spoke no Icelandic, sang no Icelandic songs, rode no Icelandic horses. Wild Olaf would have been proud of me, however, as leader of the UCLA horseback riding club leading a reckless gallop on the moonlit trails of Griffith Park.

Although I carried a heavy schedule of classes I got a part-time job as a Sunday School teacher for a confirmation class at a conservative Jewish congregation due to my extensive religious upbringing. It is an absolute truism that you never learn a subject as well as when you are preparing to teach it. Now as a university student delving into biblical history, I suddenly realized that as a youth I had accepted a series of myths and legends as sacred truths. So in the process of teaching religion, I became an agnostic.

I had had a couple of semi-serious romances in California which led to only semi-permanent commitments. The image of Dottie was like a lingering motion picture fade-out, although occasionally some haphazard thing would shock the image into Technicolor. An example is the ending of F. Scott Fitzgerald's *Winter Dreams* that I read in September of 1957: "He wanted to care, and he could not care.... 'Long ago,' he said, 'long ago, there was something in me, but now that thing is gone. Now that thing is gone, that thing is gone. I cannot cry. I cannot care. That thing will come back no more.'" And yet I still loved to verbally roll out the vibrant sound of the name Ragnheider Ingvarsdottir. People invariably smiled when they heard me say it.

I followed an accelerated study program and was graduated from the business school. The dean of the school recommended me for an position in the marketing research department of the Ford Motor Company's Edsel division, a position which was offered to me and which I accepted. There were no friends or relatives to greet me when I arrived in Detroit. I plunged into my work at Edsel working many hours of overtime but I did have time to fall in love with Vivian. It was a brief but intense affair that ended because her parents strongly rejected me since I was a Sephardic Jew, not their kind of Jew, since they were Ashkenazic Jews, a fiat to which Vivian tearfully bowed.

Dancing led to my marriage to Elaine in 1960. We both loved international folk dancing and our three children were dancing with us as soon as they could walk. Elaine was a schoolteacher who came from a non-observant Polish Catholic family and our wedding was presided over by a reform rabbi. My mother ex-communicated me and never spoke to me during the 19 years that this marriage lasted. I always left the door open for the reconciliation that didn't materialize and I grew to accept the situation with indifference. My cousin Albert in Brooklyn was the only one that continued to maintain regular contact with me during these years.

When the Edsel division downsized before its eventual demise, I was transferred to the Lincoln-Mercury division but was shortly thereafter pirated away by the Chrysler Corporation to head up a team in their market planning department. After I had been with Chrysler a year my boss Ray Ayer called me in for a performance review. He praised my work but then surprised me by suggesting that I leave the company and pursue my career elsewhere. He had been with Chrysler for thirty years and told me frankly that my future with the company would be severely limited because I was Jewish. He felt I deserved better. It was just as well for me. I had been brought up in a community where the pinnacle of achievement was having your own business. This work ethic brushed off on me. I had experienced the big corporate existence and opted out of the small cog status to become an entrepreneur.

I violated rule number one and entered a business in which I had no experience of knowledge. Overconfident, I was easy pickings for a charlatan who set me up as a distributor of an extremely overpriced line of products for institutional and industrial cleaning. But I learned my lesson fast, developed a competitive line and stubbornly persevered until I turned things around and made the business profitable. I managed this business for 31 years and sold it in 1991 for enough money to make my retirement worry free.

Within a year of the end of my first marriage I had been remarried. Susan was also a teacher and we had two children, Eve being the one who traveled with me on my return trip to Iceland. In fact, if it had not been for her suggesting the trip to Iceland this story would never have been written. I supported my other children, and Elaine and I are still on cordial terms. Susan was Jewish, which translated into renewed lines of communication with my family in Brooklyn. I held no resentment toward my mother, recognizing her conditioned response to societal pressures and shrugging the whole excommunication period off.

Since my roots had definitely been planted in Michigan, I had grown a forest of personal relationships and social activities here. Iceland had receded to an insignificant curiosity, although in my reading of travel magazines and newspaper travel sections I always clipped the rare articles about Iceland and filed them although I had no conscious plan to travel there. In the 1980s, I did read a book on Iceland by Katherine Scherman called *Daughter of Fire* which painted a knowledgeable portrait of the country.

My second marriage also ended after 19 years; I guess that's my natural limit. I do not look back on these marriages as failures, they both provided much of value but when the values played out there was a mutual agreement to bring down the curtain and move on to a new scenario. My present playbill lists many activities of choice with plenty of freedom and flexibility. My five children and four grandchildren play starring roles in this scenario and I see them regularly. Eve, who was a champion ice skater, recently moved to New York to pursue a career in dance but with the wonders of cell phones and e-mail our conversation has barely paused for a breath. When she said, "Dad, let's go to Iceland," I first thought of it as a great opportunity for father-daughter bonding. I never dreamed that I would become absorbed in a drama which has enriched my later years. The resurrection of a long dead friendship after 48 years was truly miraculous.

Chapter Fourteen
THE HEART IS A FUNNY RESERVOIR

As described in the prologue, Dottie and I had only a brief moment together in the airport at Keflavik in June 2003, before my flight jetted us back into our own separate worlds. I thought it only fair if we could add an epilogue presenting the story from the perspective of Ragnheider Ingvarsdottir. I communicated this idea to her via her sister's e-mail site. She protested that she was not a writer but that she would willingly assist me in giving her side of the story. It was a coincidence that I had planned a trip to Madrid and Barcelona for the month of October 2003, long before I had launched my summer quest for Dottie, and I knew that she also would be in Spain that month.

As October drew near I sensed a certain evasiveness on her part. In her first e-mail to me she said: *Dear Eddie, you know I'm not as young as I was 48 years ago and I'm afraid that I don't look as young as you do. Also I am ashamed that my English has not improved much with the passing years but you should know that my heart is in this letter.*

I've always been a romantic but I am not so romantic as to think that there would be a full-blown rebirth of a love that had been extinct for 48 years. I tried to tone down my approach to one of a warm but distant appreciation of our experiences together. I quoted a section from Virginia Woolf's *Mrs. Dalloway* which describes the return to England of Peter Walsh who had loved Clarissa Dallaway thirty years earlier. Peter philosophizes to himself "The compensation of growing old...was simply this; that the passions remain as strong as ever, but one has gained – at last – the power which adds the supreme flavour to existence, – the power of taking hold of experience, of turning it round, slowly, in the light."

Did Dottie feel threatened? Was I coming on to her too strongly? Did she hope or fear that I would try to renew our love affair? Her response was warm but non-committal, suggesting that I call her when I got to Madrid and saying she hoped we might meet in Spain. My next missive suggested that she accept $200 to buy a plane ticket to either Madrid or Barcelona since I owed her the money anyway for shortchanging her shopping trip in London almost five decades before. She demurred saying she could not be sure so far in advance that something might not prevent her making the trip.

> Dear Dottie,   October 18, 2003
> *I don't know exactly how to say this but I don't want you to fear me. We can be loving friends without reigniting our old relationship. We both have had full lives and we need not look back with regret on anything. I have good news for you. I have found that I can free myself on Monday, October 27th to fly down to Alicante to spend the day with you. I will call you on the phone the day before I leave the States to confirm that this will work out for you.*
>   *Your friend, Ed.*

The day before my flight I tried the phone number in Spain that had been given to me and a pitiless recording said that it was in invalid number. I tried several times with slight changes in prefix numbers but with the same results. If I couldn't call her all my plans to spend a day with her might be in vain. In desperation I searched the international phone directories on the internet to see if I could find her number there but that was also fruitless. It was then I noticed that each country had a code number and 34 was the code number for Spain that I had failed to use. I rushed back to the phone adding 34 to the string of international digits and after two rings an Icelandic-accented mezzo voice intoned, "Hello." Whew! It was all set for us to spend the day together the coming Monday but first it was necessary to overcome a couple of difficulties which suddenly arose.

The original Northwest Airlines non-stop from Detroit to Madrid that was booked was cancelled. The replacement itinerary required a change of plane in Amsterdam. In Detroit, the day of the flight to Madrid, the first plane assigned us developed hydraulic line problems, the second door problems and the third electrical problems. We took off so late that we missed the first three connections in Amsterdam. Amsterdam airport is about two miles long and I walked from one end to the other to stand in line for ninety minutes at a transfer station to be assigned a new flight to Madrid. In all it took about a full day to get to Madrid but I had come so far in time and space that I hung tough with a positive attitude. But I soon faced a second difficulty.

Madrid has a most wonderful underground metro train system. It gets you absolutely everywhere in the city fast and economically. All points of interest and spectacles always include the closest metro stop in their publicity. La Latina is the metro stop that brought me to El Rastro, the huge outdoor Sunday flea market. The guide book warned that this crowded marketplace is a haven for pickpockets. I normally avoid carrying a wallet or documents such as passports with me and this day I just slid 20 euros and a credit card in my right pants pocket. At the metro station the cars were jammed and I thought I was the last to shove my way on when suddenly someone jostled in behind me and I distinctly felt a hand sliding into my pants pocket. I quickly whirled around and struck out with my right fist. As I did so, a young blonde girl of about 18 in jeans and windbreaker drew back from me and she and a companion took off.

The public address system in the metro repeatedly warns that because the platforms are curved travelers should be careful not to introduce their feet into the gap between the subway car and the platform. When I whirled and struck out, my right foot and calf plunged deeply into this gap. I pulled myself up but in the process I twisted my left knee. The pickpocket had failed and my planned day's activities continued but by nightfall I was hobbling painfully and sleep was impossible. But Ragnheider Ingvarsdottir would be waiting for me at the airport the next morning and I would be there with or without a wheelchair.

I didn't need a wheelchair. Fortunately, the swelling in my knee lessened the next morning and I was able to walk passably well. On the plane I sat next to a portly man of about my age who turned out to be an expert on Spanish history.

"I noticed at the Royal Palace art exhibit many portraits of Carlos V and Carlos II but Carlos V ruled almost a hundred years before Carlos II. Why is that?"

"You're right, Carlos V was the great-grandfather of Carlos II. But you see he was Carlos I of Spain and Carlos V of Germany."

"I had an inkling of that already but why, here in Spain, should his German title predominate instead of his Spanish title?"

"You have a good point. Maybe we should revise our treatment of Carlos I. Incidentally, may I ask your nationality?"

"I'm a Sephardic Jew."

"A Sephardic Jew! Well you have come backward in time to your roots

The Heart is a Funny Reservoir

here in Spain."

"Yes, but I remember that you expelled my people 500 years ago and I'm still resentful."

"Don't look at me. It wasn't *my* fault."

The plane landed in Alicante according to schedule. Yes, in another sense I had come back in time. I stopped in a restroom to wash my face, comb my hair, and use a couple of Visine drops to clear my sleep-deprived reddened eyes. I had worn my black Haggar slacks with a black turtleneck, an outfit that I thought made me look fit. I chastised myself; I was not in a youth and beauty contest with Dottie but vanity is not exclusive to women. I threw my shoulders back and emerged from the airport. Two women waved at me enthusiastically. Helena, an Icelandic friend and neighbor, had driven Ragnheider to the airport to pick me up.

Helena could serve as the prototype of the new international complexion of the population in this section of Spain's Costa Blanca. She is married or, as she said, living in sin with an Italian who lived and worked in England and Iceland and now manages a restaurant in Spain. She has lived in Spain 12 years and her two young children speak Spanish, Icelandic and English. The majority of residents in this constantly growing development outside of Alicante are not Spaniards. The main bank in the town of La Marina de San Fulgencio is Deutsche Bank. The homes are populated by English, Scandinavians, Germans, French, and other foreigners. It is little wonder that Dottie has not found it necessary to develop a fluency in Spanish despite the fact that she has been spending part of her last 15 years here. I was a bit disappointed because I had hoped to chat with her in Spanish but at least her comprehension is good. Part of her daily ritual is to watch the 8 a.m. television news in Spanish.

Dottie and I spent the next six hours in constant conversation. I had brought a tape recorder so that she could tell her side of the story which appears in the epilogue to the book. I had also brought her a gift. When I was in Iceland this past summer I bought a CD record of the favorite all-time Icelandic folk songs. It had two of the songs that Dottie and I sang together way back when we sat on her slim bed in her fourth-floor room and harmonized. But she had no CD player. I was determined not to commit the same crime of omission that I was guilty of in London in 1955, and I insisted we go down to the La Marina commercial strip and find a player. We found one next to the Deutsche Bank. It was like a downsized boom box, with a vivid violet housing but it had a radio, tape and CD combination with wake-up volume.

She was tickled purple. Dottie also presented me with a touching gift. Her sister Lolly worked for a support agency for heart and lung disease victims. Lolly, herself, has suffered severe lung problems. The members of the group make a unique scarf, one side wool, the other silk, the entire silk side covered with ancient decorations found in the Icelandic sagas. My mother never succeeded in making me wear scarves, although she tried continually, but I will wear this scarf from Ragnheider Ingvarsdottir.

Dottie bought this neat home about 15 years ago in preparation for her retirement. At that time she was the first Icelander to arrive in this area, which demonstrated the courage of her Viking explorer ancestors. She is widely known and since she does not have a car she uses the buses extensively and is known around here as the walking bus schedule. We had lunch in the restaurant managed by Helena's husband where they prepared us a huge, attractive seafood paella. Dottie ate very sparingly. She has kept in trim shape and probably weighed no more now then she did in Reykjavik in the fifties. She wore beige slacks and a medium tan leather jacket.

After lunch we returned to her home jabbering all the way. The car taking me back to the airport was due at 5:30 and at 5:00 I asked if it was OK to lie down on the couch for a little rest because I had not slept the previous night. I lay down and Dottie sat near me and held my hand. And then, as if it were the most natural thing in the world, I turned on my side on that narrow couch and drew her hand to me and she slid down on the couch until our entire bodies were pressed against each other. We interlaced our legs and clung to each other joyfully. We clung together as if we were clinging to something past and irretrievable. We were a man and a woman in our seventies, who, by accepting the fates we had designed out of life, had dance stepped out of the shadows of age. Joking and giggling we vowed that neither of us had changed over the past half century. We truly believed that we had been transformed into twentysomethings and then the doorbell rang.

We stood beside the car and hugged each other probably for the last time in our lives.

"Eddie, *elsku min,* don't kiss me on the lips or you'll make me cry. I don't want to cry. I won't cry again."

The flight back was quiet and uneventful.

Ragnheider's Epilogue
HIS NAME WAS

His name was Eddie. Oh, everybody called him Ed or Sergeant Chalom but I always called him Eddie. It's like I named myself Dottie (although I spell it "Daddy") because the name Ragnheider is not an easy name to pronounce, even for Icelanders. I even gave nicknames to my two younger sisters. I called them Lolly and Holly instead of their Icelandic names and the names stuck. My brother, the youngest of us all, I named Ziggy. Maybe I just like the y sound at the end of names because it makes the person sound young and it feels more friendly.

Eddie asked me to tell my story and I told him I'm not a writer but I was willing to tell him the details and he could put it down on paper. I have to admit from the beginning that my English is not so good but he wrote out my ideas OK and smoothed out my mistakes. And you can't hear my Icelandic accent at all when you read it.

I was born in a very small village in the north of Iceland but while I was still a child my father built us a home in Hvammstangi, a much larger town of about 300 people. My father was not a farmer but worked in a sort of farmers' cooperative where the farmers brought their animals and crops for sale. My mother came from an educated family and always encouraged us to be the best we could be although I would not say that she pushed us. We were not a church-going family and the only times my mother took me with her to church was when she needed somebody to wake her up when the service was over. As a teenager I was sent away to a live-in high school which was not unusual in Iceland since there were so few children in each town. We were at home during the summertime and went home once during the school year at Christmas time. It was a strict school, the girls' building was set apart from the boys. I cannot say that I ever had a steady boyfriend in high school.

After high school, I went to an all-girls' cooking and sewing school for nine months where they taught us not only cooking and sewing but also other skills in taking care of a home and family. My mother suggested that I look for a profession. One of my aunts was a nurse and so when I was 20, I entered my country's only nursing school which was located in Reykjavik. A new student was put through a four-month trial period before being accepted for the full three-year program.

I was accepted. It was an all-female live-in school and our free time was very limited. The study program meant a lot of work. We were allowed out once a week to see a movie and one more time during the week for general free time. But accidents happen. In my second year at nursing school I became pregnant. No, I will not say anything about how this happened and who the father was. He was not any more a part of my life and never helped in the raising of my son. It was a sad and stressful time in my life and I refuse to remember or talk about things that might depress me. It would have been impossible for me to continue with my nursing training if it had not been that my parents agreed to bring up the child full time. Times had been very bad in Iceland during the war years and for six or seven years after the war. There was little work and even if you had money there was nothing you could buy. There were no shoes or stockings in the stores and we had to make our own. The soap we used in those years had such a terrible smell it made me sick in the stomach.

So I gave birth to my son in Reykjavik. The school gave me a three-month maternity leave and I took him up to Hvammstangi and then returned to complete my studies in 1953. We had a fifty-year reunion of the 1953 nursing school graduates in Reykjavik in August 2003. There were eight of us left to attend the reunion. Anyway, by 1953, things were getting better now and I was fortunate to find work in a small hospital. It was also good to have my sister Lolly, who was four years younger than me, find work in the city and live near me. I also had a first cousin named Nana who came from Denmark and lived in my building so, you see, I was not all alone. Even so, I had lived away from home for so many of my school years that I felt independent.

As a woman in her early twenties, I was interested in going out and having a good time with an eye open for the right man who might come my way and make my life complete. The Americans had come to Iceland during the war and now almost ten years after the end of the war there were still many of them stationed at Keflavik. On the weekends quite a few of them would come into Reykjavik on the bus. On Wednesday nights there was a big dance to which many of the soldiers came. I know it was on Wednesday because that was my day off from the hospital and I looked forward to the dance in the evening. During that time I went out with both Icelandic and American men but I will not admit having a preference based on which country they came from. During the year of 1955, I seemed, however, to lean toward the Americans.

I met Eddie at a dance at the Hotel Vik but I already knew his name before we were introduced. I had seen him come into some other dances with that little blonde from Hafnjarfordur a few times. He wasn't bad looking, he was almost always smiling, he was one of the best dancers, and he was a sergeant. So I asked around about him and found out that he even spoke half-decent Icelandic. At the Hotel Vik we had a chance to converse a little. So when I got the news that he had broken up with his blonde girlfriend, and since I had no boyfriend at that time, I was hoping to run into him again. I guess if you hope hard enough it works because, to my surprise, he called me up at the hospital later that week and we made a date.

We had a good time on our first date going all around town and I introduced him to some of my friends. They thought he was A-OK. And without saying anything special we understood that we would be going out together all the time. We continued to go to the dances, although I really was not a very good dancer; I had all I could do to hang on and follow him around. We also did what men and women do when they love each other, even though he always complained that my bed was not wide enough for two people. But he slept there anyway.

One day we were having dinner in the Naust restaurant.

"Dottie, have you ever been out of Iceland?"

"No."

"Iceland is the first foreign country out of the United States that I have ever been to and I was thinking that since I've gotten this close to Europe I should take advantage of seeing some of the rest of Europe."

"Where do you want to go?"

"I was planning to spend a week of my leave time in Scotland and England."

"Well, send me a postcard when you get there."

"No way."

"Eddie, why won't you even send me a postcard?"

"Because I'm taking you with me."

"You must be kidding me."

"Just get your suitcase ready, Dottie, because you're going with me."

I jumped up and hugged him but when he told me his plan I was not sure I should be so happy. He said that he would fly out of Keflavik and I would fly by myself out of Reykjavik and we would meet across the sea. My knees started shaking to think that I would be flying to a strange country alone and I had never even been in a plane before. I worried about this for days while he checked out the plans but when he finally told me he had decided that we would fly out together I let myself be completely happy.

I remember every detail of that trip, much more than Eddie does. Aside from the take-off of the plane from Reykjavik, my first scare was when we landed and we lined up to go through immigration at the Prestwick airport. The officer asked me how much money I had with me and I admitted that I had practically nothing. He asked how I expected to survive in the country without money and I just turned around and pointed to Eddie who was further back in the line. I thought for sure they were going to send me back to Iceland right then. But the immigration man went and talked to Eddie for a couple minutes and came back and stamped my passport and let me through.

Scotland was very pretty. I had never seen so many trees and bushes in my life. The inn where we stayed had a winding path that led down through a garden with flowers until it reached the entrance. It was so peaceful and relaxed after the excitement of the flight and the fright at the immigration desk. We had breakfast the next morning at the inn and spent the day on Loch Lomond. I always thought I would like to go back to that lake. The next day we went back to Prestwick for the flight to the big, big city of London. I was in the ladies' room at the airport combing my hair when they made an announcement calling for "Mrs. Chalom" because they were boarding the plane. I didn't know they were calling me. Finally, Eddie came to the entrance of the ladies' room and yelled in "Ragnheider!" and I jumped and rushed out.

The hotel in London was on Oxford Street, which was in a very nice area. I was so nervous going into that fancy lobby and walking up to the desk. The man asked me for my passport. He saw my name was not Chalom but Eddie told him that I was his fiancée and so he gave us the room key. The most exciting thing for me in London was Chinese food! They served us things that I had never seen or tasted in my life and you could eat it and it was delicious.

There were very few stores for clothes or shoes in Iceland, maybe only one store that sold shoes, and when they got in a shipment everybody knew about it and you had to get on line at five o'clock in the morning to be able to get into the store before everything was gone. Here in London there were so many stores. I bought stockings and a white skirt with wide pleats and a colored waistband. I bought it at a store called Woolworth's but I called the store Wonderful. We went to the ballet at Covent Gardens and saw *Swan Lake* and we also went to the Shakespeare theatre and saw *King Lear* with Claire Bloom playing the part of the king's good daughter. In the audience people were smoking cigars and cigarettes. The criminals and torture rooms at Madame Tussaud's wax museum were very real and very scary. We saw the Tower of London and Hyde Park, where there were so many squirrels. One night, Eddie and I went to a large dance ballroom, ten times bigger than anything in Reykjavik. There were hundreds of people dancing there. Eddie said for us to play a sort of game. I would walk around the room in one direction and he would walk around the room in the other direction and we would see if each of us could pick up someone for a dance before we got to the other side. We both did.

I go to London every year now because I have a married son with two children there. But I never forget a thing about the first time that I saw London with Eddie Chalom.

Sure, the vacation was too short but I had to go back to work and Eddie went on to Germany for a few days before coming back to Iceland. He returned and we were together again but with the trip to Scotland and London behind us I started to think of what the future before us would be. We didn't talk about the future much. I knew that he was writing to different universities and that he was going to go back to school when he got out of the Army. One day at the beginning of September he was standing in the middle of my tiny room on the fourth floor and I was sitting on my narrow bed.

"Dottie, I just received my orders yesterday to be shipped back to the States."

"When will you go?"

"Next Wednesday."

"Next Wednesday! But that's less than a week from now. I thought you soldiers stay for a whole year and I know you came to Iceland last November. I expected you would be here at least until November."

"They're letting me out two months early so that I can start my studies at the beginning of the school year in September. I'll be spending only two days at home in Brooklyn before I fly out to California to start school."

And so he was gone. I was shocked and even hurt that it had been so sudden. It was hard for me to believe that we had only been together for less than 100 days. But still I felt that in one way we had been lucky and I wrote him in Icelandic saying, "We have loved more in one brief summer than most people have loved in all their lives." How does one measure the quantity or quality of love? And maybe I have to admit that I went out with Americans more than with Icelanders with the unconscious thought that Americans had more money, could buy more things, had easier lives and wider futures. But I realized I would have gladly given all of that up. I wrote, "Oh, how I wish you were a simple *fiskimadur,* a simple Icelandic fisherman so that you could stay with me and not fly away."

But life goes on, sometimes happy, sometimes sad, sometimes just empty of all feeling. Eddie sent me a postcard from California at Christmas time with a sweet note that he wrote in Icelandic. And that was the end of everything between Eddie and me for the next 48 years. After a while, I started going out again and yes, a few years later I married an American sailor and even had a son by him, but that marriage ended after a short time and I don't want to talk about it. My two sons grew up fine. When my younger one decided to go to Sweden for medical training I went with him and ended up working at a psychiatric hospital there for 12 years. I eventually returned to Iceland where I got an apartment in Reykjavik and retired from work in 1989.

The winters in Iceland are hard and I bought a small retirement home in Spain to spend the six winter months. In June of 2003, I was on my way back to Iceland from Spain but I stopped off, as I often do, to visit with my son in London. I received a phone call from my son that lives in Iceland.

"Mama, I went to your apartment to clean things up because I know that you're coming in tomorrow."

"Thank you, dear. You're a good son."

"But, Mama, I called you to tell you there was a note left in your mailbox. It's a note from somebody who was an American soldier here a long time ago who thinks you might know him."

"Who was it? What name did he leave?"

"I can't make out the signature. It's some unusual American name."

"Is it Eddie Chalom?"

"My God, that's it! How in the world did you know?"

"I just knew."

The Loftleidir Hotel said that he had just checked out so I took a chance and went out to Keflavik airport. When Eddie came into the terminal I knew that I would have recognized him anywhere in the world. He walked with the energy of a dancer and didn't show his age. What can I say about that moment? I don't have the words.

In October 2003, Eddie came out to spend a day with me at La Marina de

San Fulgencio. I don't have a car so my Icelandic friend Helena took me to the airport to pick him up. It was wonderful remembering all we could about our past life together. Certain memories were clear for me and some that were clear for Eddie were fuzzy for me but we agreed on so many other things from those days in 1955. The hours of talking ended when the car came to take Eddie back to the airport. I was afraid he would try to kiss me. There is something so final about a goodbye kiss and I didn't want to put an end to our story. At our age we could die at any time and I refuse to end something that was precious in my life before I have to. So I only gave him my cheek. He hugged me and kissed my cheek and said *bless,* the Icelandic word for goodbye and disappeared to fly away from me for the second time in my life.

When I walked back into my empty house I noticed that Eddie had forgotten his sunglasses on the couch. There is an old Icelandic saying which promises that when someone forgets something in your house it means that he will surely return. We'll see. Miracles do happen.